SHE BETS HER LIFE

A TRUE STORY OF GAMBLING ADDICTION

MARY SOJOURNER

SEAL PRESS

SHE BETS HER LIFE
A True Story of Gambling Addiction

Copyright © 2010 by Mary Sojourner

Published by
Seal Press
A Member of the Perseus Books Group
1700 Fourth Street
Berkeley, California

Library of Congress Cataloging-in-Publication Data

Sojourner, Mary.
  She bets her life : a true story of gambling addiction / Mary Sojourner.
    p. cm.
  ISBN 978-1-58005-298-6
  1. Compulsive gamblers. 2. Gambling. I. Title.
  HV6710.S654 2010
  616.85'841--dc22
                         2009044475

9 8 7 6 5 4 3 2 1

Cover design by Domini Dragoone
Interior design by Tabitha Lahr
Printed in the United States of America
Distributed by Publishers Group West

To respect the privacy of individuals mentioned in the book, the author has changed their names.

For the Scheherazade's Sisters,
for the women who have not been
able to stop gambling,
for the women who have.

If I had one wish for women who have mortgaged their souls and traded their power for the illusion of "the big win," it would be for them to find just one person who will tell them, "Gambling is something you do, it is not who you are. You are not a worthless piece of shit; you are a person who—because you have a deadly, vicious, and aggressive disease—has made some really bad choices, and with encouragement and support, you can learn how to make different choices that will give you back your life.

—Carole Seeley, Gambling Addictions Counselor

CONTENTS

USER'S GUIDE

If you've opened this book, chances are you or someone you know may be a woman trapped in compulsive gambling—blackjack, poker, bingo, slot machines, keno, lottery tickets, craps, online gambling sites, even the stock market, or what was once a relaxing game of Bunco. And you may be seeking relief.

Welcome to my world. I have been, and I will always be, a woman one bet away from being imprisoned by a slot machine. I structured this book so a woman, her family, her partner, and her friends can easily find those sections that will be most useful.

If I'd come across this book when I was finally accepting that my gambling addiction had ravaged me, I'd have been most eager to find out that I was not alone. And I'd want hope. I played slot machines for fourteen years, the last nine years compulsively. By the time I quit, my life and nervous system were in ruins. So, I'd have gone to the Introduction, then Chapter 1: "Meet the Sisters," then Chapter 8: "A Long and Winding Road," about withdrawal.

Perhaps, unlike me, you suspect you have a problem, but you're not sure. Take a look at Chapter 2: "Crossing the Line." If you do know and are terrified by what you know, you might jump straight to Chapter 7: "The Party's Over," where you will read about how and when other women gamblers learned they had to stop. In Chapter 8: "A Long and Winding Road," you'll learn about the multitude of symptoms of both early and post-acute withdrawal syndrome. Chapter 9: "What It Takes" walks you through the resources and work of recovering *with*, as opposed to *from*, gambling addiction.

Chapter 3: "Dopamine Is Queen" is about the basics of this addiction at the level of brain chemistry and function. Chapter 4: "Freud Was Wrong" debunks early theories of gambling compulsion and sheds light on more useful and practical contemporary research and theory. Chapter 5: "Girls' Night In" brings you into a circle of recovering women gamblers as they talk about how being women impacted their gambling addiction.

Chapter 6: "Get Her to Sit Down" exposes the powerful strategies the gambling industry creates to hook compulsive gamblers and keep them playing—in the industry's words—"to extinction."

If you have already quit and are facing life without your favorite drug, read Chapter 8: "A Long and Winding Road" for the lowdown—the *low* lowdown—on withdrawal. You will learn that you have not gone crazy; you are just in the grips of a brain that longs to gamble.

Chapter 10: "The Slip" explores the reasons a woman recovering gambling addict goes back to her drug and offers strategies to prevent and interrupt a slip.

Desperate? Go directly to Chapter 9: "What It Takes." In withdrawal or in the grips of binge gambling? Go to Chapter 8: "A Long and Winding Road." You might read Chapter 3: "Dopamine Is Queen" and learn that you are not immoral, weak, or doomed. In Chapter 6: "Get Her to Sit Down," you can read about the exquisite strategies the gambling industry brings to play on a compulsive player's brain and body and know that you had help in crossing the line from fun to torment.

Bored cross-eyed by statistics? Read Chapters 2, 4, or 5 for stories from real women compulsive gamblers talking to save their lives, or Chapter 12: "Down the Road," in which you'll find the stories of women who live in gambling recovery on a daily basis.

Finally, if you are free from gambling compulsion but love a woman who is trapped, Chapter 11: "It's a Family Affair" may provide hope and the knowledge that you are not alone.

The life of a woman compulsive gambler is not a straight line, though in the worst moments of feeling trapped she may feel as though she is in a dark and endless tunnel. Life is a series of winding paths, delays, and loops. And this is where *She Bets Her Life* starts.

If you start with the Introduction, you might find yourself looking in a mirror—a mirror in which not one, but many women's faces are reflected. Some faces will be familiar, others will not. In Chapter 1, those faces might come into focus. You'll find yourself in a unique circle, a women's group of compulsive gamblers who no longer make that first bet. They are Scheherazade's Sisters. They do not tell stories to gain another day of life from a cruel husband, as in the old legend from *The Arabian Nights*. Instead, they spin out words and memories, anger and laughter, gorgeous and tattered threads of how each woman gambler is different and all are the same, into lifelines. The women tell their stories. As their words unfold, you might remember the power of story. A story can save a life.

Scheherazade was a gorgeous woman who had the bad luck of being chosen by a sultan to become his next wife. He was a whimsical fellow who married the most beautiful women of his emirate, bedded them for one night, and killed them in the morning. However, Scheherazade was no fool. The night of their wedding, she began a story for her captor—and did not finish it. She was such a wondrous storyteller that her husband was desperate to hear its end. He spared her life for one more day and one more night. Nine hundred and ninety-nine nights later, with one thousand and one stories ringing like crystal bells in their bedchamber, he knew he had fallen in love with Scheherazade and would not be able to bear living without her.

Scheherazade's Sisters was an inspired name for a group of women desperate to free themselves from a deadly addiction. Through telling our stories we began the slow, patient work of saving our own—and each other's—lives.

May this book be an invitation. May it bring you into a circle in which you or someone you love might find belonging.

She Bets Her Life is not authorized Gamblers Anonymous literature, though aspects of information and theory draw on Gamblers Anonymous's (and Gam-Anon's) twelve-step principles.

INTRODUCTION

Problem gambling is gambling behavior which causes disruptions in any major area of life: psychological, physical, social or vocational. The term "Problem Gambling" includes, but is not limited to, the condition known as "Pathological," or "Compulsive" Gambling, a progressive addiction characterized by increasing preoccupation with gambling, a need to bet more money more frequently, restlessness or irritability when attempting to stop, "chasing" losses, and loss of control manifested by continuation of the gambling behavior in spite of mounting, serious, negative consequences.

—National Council on Problem Gambling

2.7 percent of American citizens suffer from moderate (problem gambling) to severe (pathological gambling) forms of disordered gambling.

Women make up the fastest growing group seeking help for problem gambling. Women generally develop a gambling problem faster than men do. Of female compulsive gamblers, 93 percent prefer slot machines and lottery games.

—Department of Mental Health and Addiction Services
Problem Gambling Services, State of Connecticut

Stella is a tall woman. Her shining dark hair is pulled back in an elegant chignon. She wears a turquoise raw silk suit and Manolo Blahnik sandals. "Is this machine taken?" she asks. I shake my head.

She sits on the stool and sets her BlackBerry in the space between our slot machines.

"Don't you love these?" she murmurs. Stella's referring to Break the Spell, the nine-line video slot that has been hoovering up my money for the past three hours. I can tell she's going to be a talker. I consider how I might fend her off. And then I watch two little wizards fall into place on my screen, and I don't care whether she wants to chat or not.

"Oh," she says. Her voice is flat. "Lucky you. Too bad there weren't three."

I watch my credits launch. "Hey," I say coldly, "this is gonna be a $75 hit. I'm poor. That's a fortune to me." I figure that will shut her up. Rule #1: You don't comment on another player's hit—especially in a disparaging manner. Any slot pro knows that.

She's not a pro. "Oh," she says, "actually, *I'm* affluent. My husband and I are both professional psychologists. I'm in Mensa. We just do this to relax."

A year later, in 1996, I am in a Laughlin, Nevada, casino hunkered down again with Break the Spell. Someone comes up and stands behind me. It's either a novice or a slot hog with bad manners. Rule #2 of casino etiquette: Do not stand behind a dedicated player.

I turn my head. It's the affluent Mensa woman. "I know you," I say. "We were on Break the Spell in that little Apache casino."

With the opacity of a narcissist or a true slot junkie, the woman blows right by my words and snarls, "I've sunk 2,000 bucks in these friggin' machines, and *I never got the frogs once!*"

So much for Mensa, I think. *So much for affluence. So much for a professional degree. So much for relaxing.* I don't speak my thoughts. Instead I look up at her and say, "Don't you just hate that? These machines are cold as the corporation that owns these casinos."

You see, when it comes right down to it, this woman and I—and the sweet-faced old lady in the kitten sweatshirt four machines over and the giggling almost-underage Chicana behind us and the cancer-thin middle-aged biker chick yelling for a drink—are sisters in the same sorority. We are compulsive gamblers. And we are in trouble.

Seven years later, 2003, and I'm sitting with a group of women I have found through pure chance. We are all in trouble with gambling. We have no idea how to quit.

Each of us has worked all day. It is six o'clock. We are tired, hungry, eager for home and respite. And yet there is almost no place we would rather be than here—sitting on institutional chairs around a battered table in a Flagstaff, Arizona, senior center, under the chill flicker of fluorescent lights, breathing air a little greasy and saccharine with the scent of whatever the senior citizens had for their free lunch at noon.

We are here by choice and not. By bad luck and good. We've been shoved, jolted, dropped, and lifted here by grace we most often did not welcome. And we are telling stories.

A silver-haired woman, elegant and slender as an egret, begins to speak. "I'm Donna," she says, "and I'm a compulsive gambler." We know her story: a good girl from a bad family; ten years of taking care of her drunken dad and broken mother; ten years of being a mom to her four younger brothers and sisters, from the time she was eight until she fled home at seventeen; twenty-five years of taking care of a boy-man husband; a year of knowing exactly where he was while her lonely weekends dragged by, the hotel—in which he was allegedly attending a trade show, a conference, a business meeting—having no record of his registration.

We know her story, and still we listen as though each word were a revelation. "So," she says, "when I walk into a casino and see there's no one at my favorite machine, I know I'm safe in my own world. For me. Nobody wants anything from me but my money." She grins. "That's a hell of a lot more honest a deal than marriage."

Shelly nods. She's an abundant young woman, a teacher, lay preacher in her church, and caretaker for her ailing mom and developmentally disabled sister. "Being in my own world," she says, "that's what hooked me." She laughs. "It hooked $20,000 of my hard-earned cash, and 75,000 bucks from my boss." She laughs again and shoves her probation paper across for somebody—any

  SHE BETS HER LIFE

one of us—to sign. These meetings are a requirement of her probation. And checking in every day. And never ever going back into "her own world" again.

We don't find her laughter odd. We've all laughed this way. We are divas of gallows humor. The sound of the sisterhood of those who got caught and are serving time. Hard time. There is more to it. When we laugh about our gambling losses, about $500, $135,000, or in my case, who knows how much, our tired faces come alive. Our eyes sparkle. Our tense jaws relax.

You'd think we were talking about triumphs, accomplishments, good girl goals made and met. We're not. We're laughing about having gotten away with mischief—even at great financial cost.

Always, always when the laughter dies, we shake our heads ruefully. But the sparkle in our eyes does not fade. If you look closely, you see the delighted eyes of a little girl, a naughty girl, a girl whose favorite words are "You're not the boss of me."

We are, all of us, embezzlers. Either we are women who lie to our husbands or partners about the credit cards, or else, like me, we're women who embezzle exclusively from ourselves. All of us are "good" girls grown inexorably into "good" women.

We are the women you can count on to take in the lost teenage soul nobody else can stand, bake cookies at five in the morning for the VFW fundraiser, stand in the sleet in a peace demo when a president we don't want visits our mountain town. We are the last women in the world you'd expect to find on a slot machine at 3:00 AM, happily breathing in secondhand smoke and ignoring our neighbors. Should you try to chat with us, we'll snap, "Hey, I'm not here to talk. I'm here to play."

It's my turn to tell my story. "I'm Mary," I say, "and I'm a compulsive gambler." I take a deep breath. I hate saying those words, because every time I do I know my zoned-out 3:00 AMs drift further and further away. The other women wait patiently.

"I've tried," I say. "I even went to a free gambling therapy group—you know?—the one paid for by casino donations. I stayed clean for maybe three months. Then I hated being clean. Sometimes, my best friend and I would sit in the meetings till they ended at nine o'clock, then get in his truck and race to the casino. I don't know if I can stand to give my gambling up. But I might have to."

The women listen quietly.

"What hurts the most," I say, "is remembering how it feels to walk across a scorching Nevada casino parking lot, push open the smoked glass doors of my favorite casino, the Colorado Belle, and walk into a cool neon rainbow. I look at the slot machines, and I see the infinity of possibilities. It's just like Christmas morning."

I stop. I feel tears starting to form, not so much in my eyes, but from deeper within. "And Christmas morning," I say, "was the only guaranteed four hours of safety in my childhood." I hold back the tears. Every woman in the room nods. And then I say the hardest words, the ones that open out into a slow stream of tears. "I can't stand to give that up. And I can't do it without you."

Less than a year later, I had forgotten my own words. I forgot that I had lost maybe $25,000 during the long, long eight years between my first encounter with the Mensa woman and the first night I sat with other women gamblers in trouble. That's chump change for some people. For an aging woman writer who raised her kids by herself with a myriad of self-employments, it is more than a year's living expenses.

Gradually I blocked out—as many recovering addicts do—waking in terror in the early morning, brutally aware that the rent might not get paid, that a half-dozen credit card payments were late, and worse yet, that it was becoming harder and harder to find joy in my noncasino hours. I forgot the evasions I made and got away with, how bored I had become with the people I was close to, that I had stopped listening to the music that had once been my hippie lifeblood, and that I was visiting the forests and deserts that were my holy places less and less frequently.

I'd sat with the women's group for nine months when I started to feel irritated with our stories. I pulled further and further away from the other women in the group. I began to skip our circles and then to not go at all. Then, one day, when boredom was chasing itself through my mind, I said, "What the fuck!" (the addict's mantra) and drove south to a nearby Native American casino. The same old quickly became the same old.

I tried again to quit—once, twice, a hundred times. That's what compulsive gamblers do. The recidivism rate in Gamblers Anonymous is higher and more predictable than in any other twelve-step program. It seemed to be no different with the women in the gambling addiction group—and with me.

I tried white-knuckling. I tried freezing my debit card in a block of ice. I tried calling friends when I felt the urge. I tried prayer and meditation and the most widespread and respected

American addiction: being busy busy busy. No matter what I did, I could not stop playing slots.

Finally, by 2007, after years of what seemed like near-magical success as a writer and NPR radio commentator, my world imploded. I was still living in Flagstaff at the time, but everything I'd held on to as truths had altered beyond recognition: my writing and teaching career, the man I believed to be my life partner, my beloved hometown, my best friend, and the illusion that I would surf above my aging.

There was economic attrition and corporate takeover in the publishing and literary world, having to say goodbye to my former life partner for irresistible and painful reasons, the gentrification of what had been my small and friendly Western town, the damage our addictions wreaked on my relationship with my best friend. And there was the inescapable fact of my aging. It didn't matter whether the losses had come from outside or within me; they left me bitter and without hope.

But there *was* the friendly casino forty-five minutes south. There were my favorite video slot machines: Cleopatra, Sun and Moon, and Magic Mermaid. Who needed community, home, partner, or friend? I was the perfect candidate for death by Magic Mermaid.

That bleak mountain winter of 2007, ocular migraine attacks began and escalated beyond any frequency and intensity I had previously known. I'd had them throughout my life, maybe one or two a year. They begin with a blind spot, followed by an acid-bright rainbow aura that spreads across my vision and slowly fades. There are two or three hours of being unable to think clearly. It's significant that I, a woman who medicated almost anything with chocolate, hated them so much I had long ago *given up chocolate!*

I gave up aged cheese, relentlessly questioned restaurant servers about the presence of MSG in food, amped up and then cut back on coffee. The migraines did not respond to anything.

Winter slammed down with heavy snow, slick ice, and wind chills of negative ten. I decided that if I was going to be miserable, at least I could be warm. I decided to run away to the desert.

It took till spring before I finally relocated to Twentynine Palms in the Mojave. The area had long been a winter hiking and gambling paradise for me and my best friend, road buddy, and gambling pal, Everett. I left Flagstaff on April 13, a week after I lost 400 bucks in my neighborhood casino.

I figured things would be different in my new home. I'd revisit old hiking terrain. I'd walk in a new landscape, under huge sky, let the austere beauty of the place replace the clutter in my mind. I'd slow down my casino visits, get a grip, learn how to walk out of the casino with my winnings. Addiction experts call this kind of desperate move a "geographic," and they (addicts and treatment professionals alike) will tell you that a geographic doesn't work.

My geographic left me in a sixteen- by ten-foot homestead cabin, sharing kitchen and bath with my landlady—when I am both a casual housekeeper and a control empress. On May 11, I drove into town and saw that the bank thermometer read 111 degrees. A week later, a forty-mile-per-hour wind ripped a window off my tiny place. Two nights after that, something ate my beloved tabby cat, Harold.

I woke up one morning with the creepy shimmer of a migraine and began to wonder if there was something going on specific to my gambling. I found myself with that reluctant conjecture, critical for any woman gambler who wants to stop and doesn't want to stop. Soon, the migraines began to trigger panic attacks. I survived a few weeks of believing I was going crazy and then knew I needed to find a gambling addicts' support group—preferably one that was all women.

I called Donna back home in Flagstaff. She had a friend somewhere near Palm Springs who might still be part of a circle of women gamblers. "Her name's Sharon," Donna said. "Here's her cell." I called right away.

It is a tribute to their stubbornness and deep affection for their sisters-in-trouble that I found Scheherazade's Sisters still meeting, stubbornly clean, witty, and in possession of the best recipe for lemon sand tarts I'd ever tasted.

MEET THE SISTERS

The shadow on the door told Scheherazade that the king was listening. Her life would be spared only as long as she kept him listening. And so she began to weave a fascinating story web . . .

—The Arabian Nights

The Desert Hot Springs Scheherazade's Sisters feels like an echo of our little ragtag women's group back home in Flagstaff. It meets every Monday evening. There is a core group of loyalists, most of whom show up every time: Nora, Candace, Barb, Helen, Sharon, Delfina, K-Siu, and me. Other women drift in, stay awhile, then are gone. They move away, get a nighttime job, go to school. Or they aren't ready to give up their annihilating hobby.

We begin at 6:00 PM. We waste no time. We dive into a plate of sand tarts or double-deadly fudge brownies or sliced fruit (which Nora piously brings and which elicits moans of disappointment) and slam down coffee.

Then we go to work. Sometimes I'm reminded of pioneer women piecing together quilts, but instead of patching together a comforter from old velvet or new cotton, we make a crazy quilt of horror, of heartache, of the most fun we've ever had, of the maddening pain of withdrawal, and of the hard hours of slipping back. Other times we become a gang of teenage girls, full of "he saids" and "I saids." There are the nights when one of us is so filled with pain or fear that she has no choice but to sob wordlessly or tremble while the women on either side of her put their arms around her. Always, we are a circle of Scheherazades, telling stories and buying, with our honesty, a reprieve for what's left of the day, and maybe even the next.

Nobody gives advice. Nobody nags. We are too scarred and too smart for that. We talk, we listen, and sometimes we bring in new information or healing practices. I've been in the circle almost a year when Delfina comes up with an idea. "My kid just came back from treatment for *mota* . . . pot," she says. "The counselors had her write out her autobiography. I've been thinking we could do that, and one of us can read during the first half of the circle for a while."

Helen flinches. "Oh jeez. I'm seventy-two. Even if my life was boring up till I found the casinos, it'll take a year for me to read my story."

"What if," Delfina says, "we keep it to two pages. Some of us—not me, oh no—are chatty chicks, so that'll make us get to the point."

She agrees to go first the following week.

Delfina is a softly beautiful fifty-five-year-old woman. Her perfectly made-up eyes are dark, what lies behind them both warm and sorrowful. The first night she came into our circle, her eyes were only frightened. There was no delicately drawn liner, no eye shadow in shades of faintest dawn. She wore faded green sweats, and her curls were pinned up on top of her head.

Now she is the fashion forerunner of the group. Make that *found* fashion forerunner. Her gambling took her and her family down to survival level, so when she shops, it's at secondhand stores. The night she reads her story, she wears see-through plastic four-inch-heel sandals. "Turn out the lights," she says. We do. "Okay, *chicas*," she laughs. "Check this out!"

Her shoes begin to flash red and green and yellow. "They've got little Christmas tree lights in the heels. And guess what? I got them at that hospice secondhand store," she says. "Four bucks.

"Okay, now you can turn on the lights. I'm going to read my story."

I am going to use my native language sometimes in this. There are ideas that can't be accurately said in English. The most important thing about me is that I was the first one in my family—my huge family—to go to college. The least important thing about me is that I—a devout Catholic—tried to kill myself five years ago so I wouldn't have to tell my beloved viejo that I had dragged myself, him, and our three kids $75,000 into debt with no way to pay the next month's bills.

Mi madre was one of nine living children, my father one of seven. She was Mayan from Michoacán. He was third-generation American, originally from Sinaloa. They are the hardest-working people I have ever known.

We lived in South Phoenix. The neighborhood was hard, but no way the war zone it is now. I was the oldest, then came Luz, Pedro, Consuela, Miguel, and the baby, Didi. Life was good. There was always plenty to eat. I loved school. And you could still smell orange blossoms because they hadn't plowed down all the orange trees for the fancy new houses. The loss of those trees is a source of sadness to many old-time Hispanics in Phoenix.

Then, something happened. You know. That kind of something. . . . This pinche cabron, this bad, bad man and his poor, sad wife—they moved next door to us. We would hear shouting at night, sometimes screams, that awful thud of a body crashing against a wall. Maybe you don't know, maybe you do.

One day, he . . .

Delfina looks down at her hands.

. . . he got me. And he told me that if I told anybody, he would kidnap Didi and kill him before anybody knew.

So I didn't tell. Instead, I decided I would study so hard that I would go to the big white high school north of us, and then I would go to college, and I would never ever let anybody hurt a kid again.

That was all fine, but I also stopped talking. I shut myself off from my family and my girlfriends. Only La Senora, the Virgin of Guadalupe, knew what had happened. I would go to our little church and kneel in front of her, and I would pray anything I wanted. Like, "Where was your blue-eyed son when I needed him?" or "Where was God hiding?" or "Help me keep my promises to myself."

I kept my promises. When I graduated from the state university with my master's in social work, my whole family was there. I was five months pregnant, and we all went back to our little house with Elizar, my fiancé. He and I told my family that we had decided we would put the next kid in line through school. We did it. And the next. Then both of them put the next kids through.

Life was normal. I worked. My husband worked. I had two more kids. The deal is when you are Mexican there are always relatives to take care of the kids. So the kids didn't have to go to any skanky daycare center. They got love and menudo and gentle whacks on the butt. Everything was moving along right on track.

Except for the lousy dreams I had a few times a week—about the pinche cabron.

And then, some of the girls at work asked me if I wanted to go to the new Indian casino for dinner and a show. They were all giggling and teasing me about being so straitlaced. We went. My best friend sat me down at a slot machine. I never made it to dinner or the show.

What really pisses me off so bad now is that I am a substance abuse counselor. I was listening to people with troubles like ours till five o'clock, then I was out the door four nights a week to the casino. I lost ten years of my life being more estúpida than any of my clients. And the only good thing was I had stopped dreaming about the pinche cabron.

Now? I'm clean and, guess what, chicas? The pinche cabron is back in my dreams. It's a small price to pay for what I've gained, and I am thinking maybe it's time for me to face him down once and for all.

There's a long silence. Delfina shrugs. "Hey, I'm okay right now, you know?"

K-Siu looks at her gravely. "I am sad and angry to hear about that *pinche cabron*. He will come to his fate."

"Just what," Nora says, "*is a pinche cabron?*"

"A fucking butthead," Delfina says. "That's what he was, and that's what he probably still is."

"We ought to turn ourselves into guerrilla girls and track him down," Candace says. "I was lucky. Nothing like that happened to me. But I had some bad juju going for me from the time I was little, too." She volunteers to go next week. As soon as she offers this, she sighs ruefully. "Dang," she marvels, "did any of you ever notice how once you start coming to this group, you say stuff you didn't want to say? Like miss goody-two-shoes me will talk next week."

Sharon laughs. "Miss goody-two-shoes? Me, too. I used to hate women who were all goody-two-shoes. Gambling was my secret self, the tough chick whose favorite two-word sentence is *Fuck you.* Second-favorite sentence: *Leave me alone.* And now? *I'm* miss goody-two-shoes just like you. Go figure."

We circle up again the following Monday. Candace waits until we have all checked in. She's forty-two, willow-supple, her grace that of the dancer she still is—except now her dancing is in community theater rather than around a pole. The first thing you notice about her are her hands. Her fingers are long and slim. She wears a ring on three fingers of each hand. The second thing you notice are her eyes. They're black-cat green, and she doesn't need makeup. She looked good the first evening she joined us. "It's all I have left," she had said. "At least I can comb my hair and figure out what top goes with what pants. At least I can do that."

After the last of us has finished with our check-ins, Candace dives right in.

I was a selfish little bitch from the first instant I caught on that if I played cute, or sobbed real hard, or threw a hissy fit that it brought the neighbors running. My good old dad would do anything for me. I was his little princess. My mom was doing face plants in her booze— sleeping pills can keep a woman kinda drowsy. We lived in Georgia, and it was understood that women of her class were a little fragile. So, cut to the chase, I knew how to work men from the git. Then I naturally grew these tatas you see on me, and it was Miss Candace's March through Georgia.

I met Lenny. He was a professional gambler. A good professional gambler, which was about the only thing he was any good at. He sweet-talked me into running away from home. I was sixteen going on Mae West. "You've got attributes," he said, "that can make you a million dollars. But not in Macon. I've got pals in Vegas. We're heading west."

I dang near fainted the first time Lenny drove onto The Strip. It was 1983, and The Boys were stilling running the place. Out in front of the Starlite there was this peacock fan about two stories tall made out of pink and red and purple lights. I made Lenny stop the car. I got out and stood in the middle of the street and screamed, "I'm in heaven!" Nobody minded because it was about 105 degrees and I was wearing hot pants and a bikini top and five-inch spike heels.

Two weeks later, somehow, Golden Luck Lenny was broke. We were in an SRO roach hotel. And I was "Candylicious," dancing on the bar in a little mom 'n' pop strip joint. That lasted a month, long enough for me to figure out where the big bucks were—in old

*guys' pockets, just waiting for my pretty fingers to remove them. I
threw Lenny out, used what was left of my tips to buy one verrrrry
classy outfit and a pair of $90 designer pumps, and started hitting the
craps tables.*

*I met the men I wanted to meet. Let's just say I met old men,
lonely old men who never knew what hit them once Candace, South-
ern Damsel with a master's in What-You-Want, showed up. I didn't
have to do a damn thing but look at them adoringly and listen to them
natter on and on and on. I made enough with "a little help from my
friends" in the first week to get my own place and make a plan.*

Candace stops. We wait. We learned early on that sometimes a
woman's silence is as important as her words. "This gets pretty
ugly," Candace says. "I don't have to read it. It was enough to
write it, see it in my own writing, you know. See the worst of it."
She looks at Helen. "It's pretty X-rated."

"You know," Helen says quietly, "I may be an old woman
with a flag pin on her blouse and a cross on her necklace, but I
can tell you that there is more than one way for a woman to be a
paid woman. Please keep going."

"I didn't graduate to prostitution," Candace says. "In some
ways that would have been more honest." She takes a deep breath
and continues:

*Pretty soon I narrowed my area of specialization to married old
guys. I added blackmail into my trick bag. Over the next fifteen
years, I was partly responsible for at least a dozen ugly divorces and
one woman's suicide.*

I don't believe in religion, but I sure as shit believe in instant karma. I knew I had to work fast while I was still delicious. I groomed and pampered myself like the blue-blooded race filly I was. I'd put in my time till I was forty and then I'd retire. It would have been the perfect plan if I hadn't gotten bored and decided Texas Hold 'Em was my ticket to fame and more riches.

Wrong. Ten years after that sweet old guy's sweet old wife killed herself, I found myself cutting up my dead credit cards, asking a friend to take my beloved shar pei for a few days, and lying down for the kind of restful sleep you can get from a full bottle of Demerol.

Here's the instant karma part: The Demerol didn't work.

"Two out of two so far," Sharon says. "I read that the suicide rate for gamblers is higher than for any other addiction. I never tried it, but that's only because I'm a complete chicken."

"Candace, you haven't made a bet for ten years, right?" Nora asks.

"Right."

"How did you go from being a total woman-hating bitch to our sister in that time?"

"Who says I'm not still a woman-hating bitch?" Candace grins. "You ladies are the exception to the rule. You try working as a coat-check chick in a yuppie restaurant and tell me how much you like your sisters!"

We repair to caffeine and carbs. Helen has baked old-time Toll House cookies. We warm them in the microwave in the seniors' cafeteria and settle back in.

"Helen, you are a goddess," Candace says, "but that doesn't let you off the hook. I want to know what you meant by 'there's more than one way for a woman to be a paid woman.'"

"Not till next week," Helen says softly, "I'll read my story next week."

Delfina calls me a couple days before the next meeting. "Would you talk to Helen? She called me. She's having a terrible time writing. I figured maybe, you being a writer and all, you could help her."

Helen picks up the phone on the second ring. "Mary, I am so sorry. I feel like such an idiot. I can't do this."

"You don't have to," I tell her. "It's only supposed to be a tool."

"I do have to do it. You don't understand. I'm the oldest person in the group—five years older than you even. Sometimes I listen to all of you and all I can think is that the only interesting thing I ever did in my life was hitting that $5,000 progressive jackpot on Wheel of Fortune. I have to write this, or I'll feel like an old fool."

"Do you want me to help? I used to teach writing. It's probably the one thing I'm not scared of."

There is a pause. "We could do that. The sooner the better."

An hour later, Helen and I are sitting on her patio in the shade of a lush clump of yucca. The scent of flowers fills the air. A small fountain trickles into a shining koi pond.

"I did all of this," Helen says. "My husband thinks it's a waste of money, but I needed something for my soul."

She pauses. "My soul. I'm beginning to understand that my gambling hurt my soul. Do you know what I mean?"

I look into her kind face. I know we might have hugely different definitions of soul. "I do know."

"So," Helen says, "can you help me write these impossible two pages?"

"I will. We need paper, a pen, and a kitchen timer."

When she returns I say, "Here you go. You set the timer for twenty minutes. I'll give you an opening sentence. I'll start the timer, and you'll write. No matter what, keep the pen moving. If you get stuck, just write something like 'I can't do this. I'm stuck. I hate Mary. I'm leaving.' Anything, but just keep the pen moving. Here's your opening sentence: 'I have my own story to tell.'"

Twenty minutes later, Helen indeed has the beginning of her own story to tell.

"What next?" she says.

"I leave. You set the timer, and you write the next section."

Helen calls that night. "Now what do I do with the ten pages I wrote?"

"Take out the scalpel," I say, "and cut away everything but the soul."

The Helen who walks into the next meeting of the Sisters is not quite the Helen we'd known before. She sits in her chair quietly and waits instead of making sure each of us has coffee just the way we like it and more than enough cookies.

We fill our plates and cups. Sharon brings Helen a cup of tea. Cookies have been off-limits for Helen for ten years because of late-onset diabetes. She never complains. And when it is her turn to bake, the cookies are anything but low-carb.

Helen has described herself to us as "a medium woman—medium weight, medium height, medium wrinkles, medium gray hair, medium aches and pains, medium except in how I, well you know, went nuts with those damn machines."

We do our check-ins. Candace finishes last and nods at Helen. "Break a leg."

Helen smiles. "Feels like I already did. Here goes."

I have my own story to tell. It's most likely different from you girls', partly because I'm seventy-two, but even more because I'm a country Okie, born, raised, and bred. I've noticed most of you come from cities or suburbs. When I was born there were no such things as suburbs, especially not in Sallisaw, Oklahoma. It was 1935, and we were maybe seventeen hundred folks, mostly cotton farmers, a few loggers and miners . . . and their families of course.

My pop ran a little café. My mom ran us. Till she took sick with lung fever. I was the oldest of six kids, so at nine I became the second mom. We got hit bad by the Great Depression. My pop was able to hang on. Besides the bakery, his café was the only place to get a decent meal. He and my mom knew how to squeeze a nickel till the eagle hollered and how to make home-fry potatoes and onions that folks swore were better than a whole Thanksgiving dinner.

Hard as times were, we were a proud family in a proud town. When that John Steinbeck wrote his book about Okies and the Dust Bowl, a lot of Sallisaw got plain irked. He claimed the Joad family was from Sallisaw, and that was nonsense. We didn't have a drought, and we were the hardest-working people you'd have ever met.

Now, that bank robber, Pretty Boy Floyd, got buried in Sallisaw. I wasn't born yet, so I didn't get to go, but there were twenty thousand people at the funeral. My pop made out like a bandit himself, what with people getting all worn-out from the excitement and needing a decent meal under their belts.

That was the last real excitement Sallisaw had till Bill Hedge put in his racetrack, Blue Ribbon Downs, in 1960. You couldn't legally bet on the races, but I can tell you there were plenty of deals going down in my pop's cafe.

My mom died when I was twelve. I had my hands full. It looked like I was going to turn out to be one of those old maids no girl in her right mind wanted to be. Besides, we were hard-shell Baptists, and my pop was right fussy about any boy being good enough for his girls.

Till a new blacksmith came to town, set eyes on me slicing up pie in the café, and that was all she wrote.

I married Jim Brooker, had five kids, and was a faithful member of my local church. The only gambling I'd done—and I didn't count it as gambling—was Bingo Night at the VFW hall. Then the Ladies Auxiliary decided to go to the buffet over at the brand-new Choctaw Casino. I was a grandma twelve times over by then and a great-grandma of three. Jim was retired. It was 2005. You should have seen us girls. We got all dressed up and decided that if we gambled, we'd each play $20 apiece and put what we won in the Widows and Orphans fund.

None of us had ever gambled in a casino before. I didn't know then that going to bingo every Thursday night, rain or shine, sick with a cold or not, counted as gambling. My Jim used to play the ponies, and rumor had it that May Jenkins's husband, Bill, had gotten himself in a little trouble with poker up in Tulsa. But we were good

Baptist ladies, so the most fun we ever had involved chocolate or a hand of bridge. I didn't much like the slot machines that first night. Seemed like a bad bargain. Bingo was a lot more fun.

But then a few weeks later, I was home with Jim driving me nuts—what is it about men and retirement? He'd never taken an interest in anything I did till he got his gold watch. All of a sudden he was an expert on my cooking, washing clothes, mopping, dusting—without doing any of it, I might add. I told him I was going down to the library to take a computer class. He grunted, and I was out the door.

The only computer I set eyes on that day and many days after was a slot machine.

Between tornadoes, winter temperatures of negative fifteen, and the worry about my husband finding out about the secret casino hours of my life, I was only too happy when he suggested it was time for us to head west. We picked up a nice older double-wide in Desert Hot Springs in 2006. For a while, I was happy just to get settled in, plant a garden, play a little bingo at the Catholic Church, and learn how to email my Sallisaw girlfriends.

Then May and a couple other gals paid a visit. They were all sparkly-eyed when we picked them up at the airport. They were like kids with a secret. Only later, after Jim had settled in with his football game, did they drag me out to the patio and show me a flyer from the big casino in Palm Springs.

That was the beginning of the next beginning of the end. You know the rest of the story.

"Excuse me," K-Siu says, "I don't mean to be rude, but where is the part about you?"

Sharon nods. "I know more than I ever guessed I'd know about Sallisaw, Oklahoma, more than I care to know about Jim, and not enough about when you were little or young or middle-aged."

"There was no part about me," Helen says, "until I really started to gamble. Up until then all I was about was my husband, my kids, my grandkids, my great-grandkids, the Ladies Auxiliary, and my sick mom. I couldn't have told you what color I liked, the last book I read, or even what color my eyes were. I remember the time I walked into that fancy casino and saw the empty seat at my favorite slot machine and thought, *This is all mine. Just mine. There is nobody else but me here.*"

Helen pauses for a moment and adds, "That me is gone now, too. I kind of miss her. She was funny and mean, and she knew how to have fun. But there's more of me now, since the year I've been meeting with you ladies, than there was in seventy-two years of my life."

"So what about your favorite color, a book you've read, and your eyes?" Barb asks.

"My favorite color's blue-green, I read a whole Margaret Coel mystery last week, and my eyes are cloudy gray."

"I still want to know what you meant," Candace says gently, "when you said that there's more than one way for a woman to be a paid woman."

Helen's faint smile is pure ice. "I can't believe I'm going to say this. Imagine sleeping with a man you couldn't stand for thirty-nine years—because you needed the security."

She pats Candace's hand. "You see, there is more than one way for a woman to earn her keep."

Let's take our break," Helen says, "that wore me out."

We are closing the circle when K-Siu blurts out, "I will go next. I am a little like Helen. I, too, come from people who lived in a small village. My people are traditional and religious. But I'll tell the rest next week."

The night of K-Siu's reading she wears a long, high-necked satin dress, slit to the knee in the same scarlet as her precious rubies.

"I wear an *ao dai*," she says. "It is not my native clothing because the skirt and blouse and headdress my mother brought over from Vietnam were taken by the people at customs. We never learned why."

K-Siu is a short, sturdy woman with warm, dark skin and mahogany eyes. She is forty-two, the mother of three. She always wears a gold charm bracelet with six rubies hanging from it.

"These are for my mother, my father, my husband, and for Nicky, Wynne, and William." She waits till we are all settled in, then she begins:

I am not Vietnamese. I am Bru. My mother and father taught us as small children that we were not Vietnamese. We were Bru. My people are one of the tribes of the Degar. We are highland dwellers—what's left of us. The French called us Montagnards. We call ourselves Degar. It means "sons of the mountains." My name is not Bru. It is the name of a Degar nurse who was buried alive by the South Vietnamese just before the American War ended. My mother and father taught us that to remember our people is the essence of being Degar. They were from the village of Lang Troai on the Sepong River at the border of Vietnam and Laos. We do not know if the village is still there. So many were destroyed in the American War and after.

Gambling has always been a tradition in our family, as it is for many Degar and Vietnamese. Because I grew up in the States, I don't know much about the games the men played back in the village, but we follow the Vietnamese custom of gambling at Tet, our New Year. We play Bau cua ca cop, a dice game. The dice are very beautiful, not like the numbered ones. The six sides of the dice have pictures of a fish, prawn, crab, rooster, calabash gourd, and stag. Sometimes I dream of them. And of my parents' hands holding them.

And there is an old game, the same as keno here. My mother laughs when she hears one of her friends wants to go to the casino to play keno. "Not keno," my mother says, "White Pigeon Ticket. The game has been called White Pigeon Ticket for hundreds of years. Then, white pigeons; now, sparkly lights and buzzers."

For most of the Bru I think gambling was just a game, but the Vietnamese regard gambling as the worst vice among the four vices of womanizing, drinking, taking drugs, and gambling. I tell you these things because to tell of my life is too hard. And I want you to know that always, for me, gambling was like the yin and the yang. There were the beautiful dice of Tet, and there are the ugly effects of what I did.

Bru are not Buddhists. Some are Christian, many were and still are people who believed in the spirit in everything. But we also believe, as the Buddhists do, that what we do has consequences. And we cannot outrun those consequences. I live with the consequences of my foolishness every day.

I have told you about my sadness over the loss of my husband. I caused it with my love of the dice and White Pigeon Ticket. I have not *told you of the loss of my mother and father. Not because they died or chastised me in any way. They are alive and as kind as they have ever been, but now my secret lies between us, the secret of their good daughter and what she did to support her gambling habit. Now when we talk on the phone, or email, I am not myself. I do not tell them the truth.*

I can't write more.

The group is silent. K-Siu sits calmly with her hands folded in her lap. And then she says, "If you want to ask me questions, I can try to answer them."

I half expect one of us to ask her about what she had done that had left her with so much shame, but that is because I have forgotten we do not pry—ever.

"I wonder about one thing," Nora says. "What is the meaning of the white pigeons?"

K-Siu smiles. "White Pigeon Ticket was a kind of lottery. It began in China long ago. Gambling was outlawed there, so the gamblers set up their shops in the countryside, where the police could not find them so easily. The city gamblers made their bets on paper tickets, tied them to the legs of white pigeons—our homing pigeons—and set them free. The pigeons carried the bets to the gambling shops. After the lottery numbers had been drawn, the gambling shops sent word to the winners by pigeon. I used to imagine the pigeons wobbling home because they would have so much paper money wrapped around their legs."

Delfina laughs. "My husband and his brothers keep pigeons for racing—and betting. I tease him about it, but he and I both know I have the gambling virus and he doesn't."

We move on to telling how our weeks have been, what has been hard, what has been easy. At the end of our time, Nora says, "I'll go next week. I need to get it over with."

The next week Nora races in the door at the last minute. "I'm so sorry," she says, "but Sarah came down with a stomach bug, and Jen was late coming home from work, and by the time we got it all straightened out, I had twenty minutes to get here, and the traffic was insane."

Nora is a sturdy thirty-two-year-old redhead who lives with her partner, Jen, and Jen's daughter, Sarah. She's an endearing mix of radical chic and practical. She's wearing her John Lennon granny glasses and a long, flowered skirt along with her favorite Carhartt carpenter's vest and skateboarding sneakers. She's a woodworker, both parquet and fine cabinetry. And she is quick to show off the Lesbians Love Lucy button on her backpack.

She grabs her two basic food groups, ginger dreams and coffee, and settles in to read:

The best way you could describe Scheherazade's Sisters is a blend of old-time consciousness-raising group, old-time twelve-step meeting, and United Nations, where I'd be the representative of Gayavania.

You'd be surprised how many of us enlightened, political lesbians are gambling junkies. I'll never forget the time I snuck off to my favorite gambling haunt, quaint little Laughlin, Nevada; was snuggled down with my favorite poker machine; and heard all this shrieking coming from the escalator.

Two busloads of queers and dykes from Tucson had just rolled in. I hit Max Bet and watched the ace, two, three, four, and five of spades unfurl on the screen. I figured I had died and gone to heaven. However many hours later, it was the middle of the night, and I just figured I had died.

There's an old joke you used to see written on the stalls of ladies' rooms: "My mother made me a lesbian."

"Cool! If I give her some yarn will she make me one, too?"

Nobody made me a lesbian. I was born with the gift. And nobody made me a gambler. I figure I was born with the curse. My family is totally cool, liberal Unitarian, Mom and Dad married for forty years, Mom and Dad both work, but Mom raised me and my sister and brother at home till the oldest was five. No creep ever touched me. No mythological butch gym teacher ever lured me into the shower. All I know is I remember being four years old in preschool when the new kid, Janey Whatever, walked in and I couldn't breathe.

In case you don't know, not being able to breathe is the first sign of a fatal romantic attraction. I didn't even know there was anything weird about how I felt. I drew a beautiful black horse on a piece of paper and gave it to her. That was the extent of the romance.

I didn't think it was weird either when I was in fifth grade and found a gang of boys who played poker for money once a week. I was the only chick. The first second Ricky dealt me my cards, I had that same out-of-breath feeling, and the first time I bet 5 bucks, I thought I was going to suffocate. I should have paid attention.

Down the road, being gay saved my life and my heart; gambling nearly burned them to a crisp.

I've worked since I was twelve. I grew up in a suburb that was going global. I'd hang out on the construction sites and do anything

I could do. The guys—they were all guys back then—let me gofer beer and smokes at the convenience store up the road while they were working. They'd tell me to keep the change. Pretty soon a few of them started teaching me stuff. I learned how to pound a nail, how to measure and cut, how to make mitered corners that were waterproof. One of the guys taught me some fancier stuff: inlay, burning designs into the wood, hand-carving a flower into a door pull.

By the time I was sixteen, I was working part-time for a crew that put custom cupboards and doors into otherwise-cheap-shit trophy mansions. By the time I was eighteen, I had my own crew. We specialized in projects no other crew would take on. And we specialized in two-hour lunches of taco cart nutrition, beer, and poker.

I quit the beer and the poker when I met Jen. I was twenty-six. She was thirty. She had a kid, Sarah, who I've adopted. Everything was great for three years. Then the local tribe built a casino ten minutes from our home.

I started out with poker, loved Texas Hold 'Em. Then, as the jones advanced, poker was too slow. So I slid myself right down the social scale of gamblers and began to hit the slots.

Nora pauses. She pulls a wad of slot cards out of a vest pocket, a pair of scissors out of her pack. "I didn't write this part of my story, because I just wanted to say it—and here I go!" She takes the first card and cuts it into strips. Barb pulls the wastebasket over. Nora drops the strips into the basket, takes the second card, and slivers it.

"I've been coming here for two years, but I just couldn't bring myself to cut up these cards till after I wrote my story and got my butt in here tonight."

She drops the last plastic shard into the wastebasket and shrugs. "There! That's all she wrote."

We applaud. Nora takes a little bow.

Sharon and I flip a coin to see who will go next. I win. "Guess it's me," Sharon says, "but aren't we supposed to count that as gambling?" It's one of the few times a Sister gets booed.

The following week, Sharon pulls two neatly written pages out of her leather purse. She brushes a strand of silver-white hair away from her eyes and grins. She is the epitome of careless class. Whenever I see her I think of how people say that Parisian women can toss on a T-shirt and jeans and look more elegant than *any* woman in formal wear. Sharon is forty-nine with the body of a healthy thirty-year-old. We all work hard not to hate her.

"I love what I'm going to read," she says. "I actually wrote it before as part of a longer bio when I was in treatment. The rest of my history is pretty dull preppie, so I figured you'd rather hear this. It's really about a woman helping another woman—almost unintentionally, just because she's being friendly. I try to remember that kind of helping now.

"This may seem weird, but my story's in third person. I was so ashamed those first months in treatment that I needed to work out some things this way."

Nobody knew. Not her husband. Not her boss. Not her minister. Not her therapist. Certainly not her kids. Not even Ramon, her warm and irreverent hairstylist, who knew about everything else.

Only Sharon had begun to suspect she could no longer pretend she didn't suspect.

She might have held on to her lonely and terrifying knowledge forever had Ramon's nail technician not talked her into a new shade of polish. Sharon had always gone with sedate. Pale beige-pink, maybe something a little brighter if there was a special party. But when Amber showed her the tiny French bottle—Cinnabar—and Sharon saw how the dark mineral red made her pale skin elegant, she told Amber to go ahead.

Five hours later Sharon was at the casino. She'd told Bob she had to work late and that she'd left a bowl of pasta primavera in the fridge for him and the kids. As always, he said, "Got it covered, babe," and that was that.

Sharon decided to try a new machine. She'd had her eye on a twenty-line penny slot with alluring sun and moon symbols that gleamed as they signaled a bonus. She took $100 from the ATM and settled in.

By 11:45, Sharon had maxed out her available withdrawals from her debit card: $500. She made herself go to the snack bar for a yogurt, forced herself to swallow the gooey stuff, and knew enough not to order the coffee she badly wanted. She might leave. She might drive woozily home. She might remember she had a 7:00 AM meeting the next morning. She would have to sleep, and even the bad casino coffee would tap-dance in her head.

She went back to the ATM and slid in her card. Funds unavailable at this time. Bob must have paid some bills.

She slid in the blue card. Nothing. The shiny silver card. Nothing. Finally, she slid in the high-interest card she'd surreptitiously ordered from a magazine. Nothing. She could feel someone standing behind her.

"Whoa," a young woman said. "Outrageous."

Sharon turned. "I'm okay," she said. "I'll just be a second. There must be a computer error. Or maybe I just have to wait till midnight."

The woman looked puzzled. "No," she said. "I'm not in a hurry. We both gotta wait till midnight anyhow to take out more money. I was just watching your fingers. That polish completely rocks."

Sharon looked down at her hands. To this day, she has no idea why what came next arrived. She saw her five fingernails gleaming in the neon. She saw her hands. She thought of all the other ways she used them, and she put the last credit card back in her purse.

"Thank you," she said. "It's called Cinnabar. My nail technician turned me on to it."

The girl nodded. "Listen," she said, "you look a little funny. Are you okay?"

"No," Sharon said. "Not really."

And that was the beginning of the end.

Sharon left the casino. The air outside was filled with exhaust from the cars pulling in and out of the parking lot. She looked up past the big, gorgeous sign. She couldn't see a damn thing of the night sky.

She drove home, and for a week she didn't say anything to anybody. And then, she made an appointment with Ramon. He would be the first to know. It would be a long time between telling Ramon and telling another person, and even by then, she wouldn't be sure she wanted to stop.

There's her story. And it's all mine.

"Where's Ramon at?" Candace says with sisterly compassion. "I've always loved your hair!"

"That's my deepest, darkest secret," Sharon says. "He's already booked to the tits. He'd love me saying that. Pretty boring deepest, darkest secret for a woman who once considered herself a chick outlaw gambler."

We finish out the meeting. "You're next," Sharon says. "But I think you should have to say it rather than write it. You know how you writers are."

"We're professional liars," I say. "I'll just improvise."

I hadn't shared with the circle that I can speak publicly as easily as I can write, but the night it's my turn I seem to have forgotten everything I know about just letting go and letting the words happen. I sit in three chairs before one of them feels remotely comfortable. Barb brings me a cup of decaf. "You don't need high octane," she says, "you're jittering so much the chair is bouncing." She and the others sit down.

"Okay," I say, "I'm starting," and promptly feel myself begin to get emotional. "Okay," I say. "Now I'm really starting." I choke back my tears. I can't remember the last time I cried. "Any second now," I say. My voice shakes so much I can't do anything but shut up.

Candace hands me a tissue. Sharon puts her arm around me. K-Siu sits across from me and looks calmly into my eyes. "Okay!" I say. "Here I go." A few minutes later I'm finally able to speak.

When I was five years old I was alone with my mother when she had her first psychotic break. No, wait, first off, I am a classic addict:

Anything I like I want more of till it stops working or near kills me. There's a great Guns N' Roses lyric about how you start out with a little just for fun and that the "little" gets huge.

This is how I became a classic addict as best as I can piece it together. Let's go back to the little girl kept home from kindergarten because her mom was afraid to be alone. She's in her parents' big bed because that's what you get to do when you stay home from school. You get tomato soup and peanut butter toast, and your mother puts on the radio, and together you listen to soap operas. Except this time, there was no radio coming from the kitchen. Instead, there was just a crazy singing that sounded like it was coming from a monster.

I had a coloring book in my lap. I didn't read yet. So there was this terrible monster singing in the kitchen where my mom was supposed to be. Footsteps started coming toward the bedroom. I knew my mom had turned into that terrible monster.

Here's where playing slots comes in. I heard the footsteps, and all I could think to do was look down really hard at that page in the coloring book, and when it didn't make what was happening go away, turn the page like a little robot and stare down at that page, and then the next.

I was five, and I had already taught myself to go away from reality into something I was staring at. Once I could read, I graduated to books. Once I could date, I got a PhD in my boyfriend's face.

The second training I got in being an addict was having serious asthma in the 1940s. The doctors didn't know much. So I spent days, weeks propped up on pillows in bed and making myself take every single breath. There was not a breath I wasn't aware of.

So I learned how to go away, and I learned how to be compulsive. Being able to do those two things saved my life as a child. It wasn't just carefully watching my mother to see if she was starting to slip, but I also had asthma for many years and many times had to concentrate on every painful breath I drew. My obsessiveness and compulsivity make me the writer I am. I can't let a sentence go if it isn't right. In a strange way, obsession and compulsion can be skills—maybe even lifesavers.

And I can't think of a better place to hone those two skills perfectly than sitting on a stool in front of a slot machine screen.

The only comforts in all of this are that now I suspect that gambling compulsively gave me a place to retreat from crippling anxiety so that I could stay alive and write, and I've learned that only through finally getting clean was I able to access the reality of my mother's illness and my terror. Another comfort of being clean is that I called my brother, from whom I had felt estranged for years, and he corroborated what I had realized—and now we are finally true sister and brother.

I look up. Barb's face is pale. She says, "I had a crazy manic speed-freak dad. He got better for many years, but now—he has Alzheimer's, and I'm the only one to take care of him.

"It's my turn next week. I'm glad to go last because now I don't feel so weird and alone."

We break out more cookies and coffee. I dive in and restore my electrolyte balance, but even before the sugar kicks in, I am surprised by how much better I feel.

Barb leads off the next week. She is 41 going on 141. Most of the time, her eyes are tired, her natural blond hair is pulled back in a straggly ponytail, and her clothes are basic. "I have six variations on this stunning outfit," she has told us. "Sweatshirt and pants in blue, gray, black, red, green, and baby-food-stained pink." But on the night she reads her story, she wears an ivory silk blouse, dark brown jacket, and dark brown short skirt that shows off her fabulous legs.

"I got dressed up," she says. "This suit's a little back-dated, but I haven't bought real clothes in ten years. That's what I loved most about online gambling. Nobody cared what I looked like. Nobody wanted a damn thing from me but my money. When they built that casino in Indio and I caught on that my casual wear was damn near formal compared to everybody else, I was even happier.

"Here goes":

I was two weeks pregnant on my graduation night. I was chosen for the Senior National Honor Society, the DAR Good Citizen Award, Most Likely to Volunteer Their Brains Out Award (I made that up), and was 10th in a class of 285. I was Danson, Barbara. My boyfriend was Davidson, Jon. When we waited in line to go up on the stage, he whispered to me, "Hey, hot stuff, if they only knew what we were doing last night."

A girl with a crazy dad is going to go to whatever shelter she can. Jon's arms were all the haven I had ever dreamed of. Until I was three months pregnant and he finally caught on.

No way was I going to have an abortion. Not for moral reasons, but my mom had told me horror stories. You know, blood-soaked mattress, all of that.

So Jon and I got married. I had the kid, then the next two kids. Then Jon decided he needed to find himself. Ho hum. And I decided he needed to find himself anywhere but near me.

Cut to degree in library science. Cut to working mom. Cut to working mom who cannot, CANNOT not see when something isn't fair. You know, once a good citizen, always a good citizen. So, working as a Bookmobile lady, volunteering as PTA president, program chairman at my church, Food Bank clerk twice a month, and warm 'n' cozy home-on-the-block for all the waifs in the neighborhood.

Cut to I'm messing around on the computer one night, and I find a place where you can play free online poker. I fool around for a few months. It eases my mind, relaxes me so I can go to sleep without Xanax. I get pretty good and think, *Hey, why not play for money?*

It goes pretty easy for a while. I keep myself under control, start in around nine and play till midnight because I have to get up in the morning to drive the Bookmobile. Then, something happens. More like, some things happen.

I manage to find time to fall in love with one of my neighbors. He's recently divorced and horny as I am. I forgot to mention that part about me. We go at it whenever we can. Sometimes we use protection. Sometimes not.

One night, as I've just watched the cyber-dealer give me a straight flush, it dawns on me that I am feeling uncommonly good for a gal who should be having PMS. Three weeks later, I find out I'm pregnant. Three months later, a stranger calls to tell me that my father has been found wandering in Trader Joe's, insisting that somebody show him where the naked hula ladies are.

A day later, I am picking my dad up from the emergency ward, pulling over, locking him in the car, and puking into any bushes that happen to be alongside the road.

A year later, the new baby is bunking with my last almost-grown-up kid at home, Dad is in what was the laundry room, and I have quietly removed $10,000 or more from the state PTA treasury, found an adult care service that will daddy-sit at my home, and acquired my matching sweatshirt outfits for 10:00 PM runs to the local casino. I learn that my outfit and my generally haggard aspect work great—when they work—at the poker table. And then, I decide to try the slots for a change of pace.

The new baby goes colicky, Daddy eludes the adult care worker every other day, I begin to notice that the book titles in the Bookmobile have gone blurry, my horny neighbor goes back to his wife—and I don't care. You all know. The instant those smoked-glass casino doors open and I am in, there is no other shelter I would ever want. I start dipping into the unusually ample PTA—$12,000 altogether.

How I quit? I got caught.

Sharon begins to laugh. "What's funny?" Barb snaps.

"You," Sharon says, "c'mon, you know how funny you are, but that's not why I'm laughing. I'm laughing because my husband and I day-traded for months online, and it never occurred to me till now to consider it gambling.

"Oh yeah, both of us in our flannel jammies, ice-cold martini pitcher, maybe a line or two of blow. It was heaven in the privacy of home."

"It was so easy," Barb says. "I could gamble till my eyeballs spun. The baby was safe. My dad was zonked out in his room. I had my diet soda, my pizza, and my double-fudge ice cream only a few feet away in the fridge. It *was* heaven." She gets that thousand-yard stare.

"So," I say, "would you have stopped if you hadn't been caught?"

Barb shakes her head. "I don't know. I'd be lying if I said anything different. But I did get caught. And, for right now, I haven't made a bet. That's going to have to be good enough."

I know exactly what she is talking about. And, as close as anyone can come to feeling another person's emotions, I know damn well how she feels.

A week or so after we finish our stories, I tell the circle that an idea has managed to finally make its way through the sludge of my gambling withdrawal.

"Being with all of you has made me realize that I want to give back what I'm learning. I want to help some woman who's in as deep shit as I was to know she's not alone—or going crazy. My withdrawal was so bad I thought I had Alzheimer's. I couldn't find one scrap of information on the symptoms of gambling withdrawal—not in books, not online, not from my counselor at the time. I was terrified.

"I want to write a book about women and compulsive gambling. I'd like to use us and our stories as the heart of it, include your autobiographies in your own words—that way the women who read the book might find pieces of themselves in your stories."

There is a spooky silence. Helen shakes her head. "Not my stories," she says. "No way I want the other folks in my trailer park to know what I've been up to."

K-Siu frowns. Barb looks away from me. I look around the circle and know my brilliant idea might be dying before it even has a chance to formulate in my mind.

Candace laughs, "I don't give a shit. My life's an open book. Between my busy booty and how guys talk, everybody in this town knows Miss Candace's business."

Sharon looks at me. "Maybe you could tell us more. Are you going to use exactly who we are and what we say?"

I feel my breathing resume. "No. How could I? I'll change our names. I'll change the place. I'll change everything but my story. . . . "

"To protect the anything-but-innocent," Candace says. "Cool."

We talk the rest of the evening. By the time the coffee and blueberry pie are gone, each woman has agreed to let me use her words—more than agreed. Candace sums it up for all of us when she says, "If my story can help one woman before she gets in over her head—or even after she does—that'll be enough for me."

CROSSING THE LINE
HOW A WOMAN KNOWS SHE'S HOOKED

You can fool a fan, but you can't fool a player.
—1970s street wisdom

There is a moment for each of us in Scheherazade's circle when we've said to ourselves, "I can finally remember when I crossed the line."

When we talk about this in the group, every woman nods. "Crossing the line" is the moment or moments when you realize there's been a priority shift—when you're playing a slot machine, watching the roulette wheel spin, holding your breath while the dice fall into place, spending half the grocery money on lottery tickets; when stealing a minute, an hour, an afternoon from your boss to check your stocks goes from being fun to being the raw necessity for staying alive. In fact, risking your money has become the only necessity.

"I played out my last buck at the blackjack table," Candace says. "Credit cards tanked; my pal the pit boss just shook his head when I asked for another marker. I was over my ATM limit till morning. I felt like everybody was watching—and feeling sorry for me. I scrounged in my purse. Four pennies. And these days you can't put the actual coins in slot machines, so that was it."

At that point she turns to us and says, "I got up and had to grab the machine to steady myself." Candace is the one with the dancer's lithe body. She's hardly a feeble woman. She laughs. "You know—how your legs go numb? I pretended I had bumped my foot on the stool. I couldn't bear to look at the people on either side of me."

"As if they gave a damn," Nora says. We all laugh.

"Yeah," Candace says, "I was past thinking. I remember walking past the security guard and recognizing she wasn't the same person who'd been there when I came in. And then, all of a sudden, the smoky air seemed unbearable. I pushed through the doors, and damn me if the sun wasn't coming up behind the mountains. I remember a thought, more like a ghost of a thought, flitting through my mind. *I am in deep trouble.* But then I realized I had a two-hour drive to get to work and one hour till I was due for my shift, and I didn't have time for belly button gazing. It was five years before I could look back and see the line that was only a shimmer that morning."

"Isn't it strange," Barb says, "that you knew and you just blew by it? I did the same thing. In fact, I probably thought, *I'm in deep trouble* a hundred times. But then I'd hit a jackpot, or I'd make it home okay, and the next morning I'd figure out how to cover my ATM withdrawals, and I'd forget."

"I knew I was hooked years before I finally walked in here and said, 'I'm addicted to gambling,'" I tell the group. "I just didn't care. It was the most fun I'd ever had. I figured it was a way to get old. A woman's desirability is doomed, but a great slot machine doesn't care whether I look like a shar pei. All it wants is my money. That's a clean deal compared to dating most men my age."

Nora punches me on the arm. "You go, Feminist Hag."

Sharon laughs. "De-Nial, that river we love to float on. I had more than a few moments when I knew I'd crossed a line, but like you, Mary, I got past them. It'd be 4:00 AM, I'd have maxed out my credit cards, the pit boss wouldn't hold one more marker for me, I'd have a flash of sanity wondering what my husband would think, and I'd hyperventilate so bad that I even passed out one time and woke up in the security office with a guard handing me a paper bag to breathe into. But then I'd remember a twenty I'd stashed in the glove compartment, and that my husband had his own hobbies, and that I hadn't yet dipped into the money market fund I'd inherited from my grandmother—so how far gone was I really? And then I'd feel as perky as I had when I'd walked in the casino twelve hours earlier."

"It wasn't that much fun for me," K-Siu counters. "It wasn't fun at all. Because no matter what I knew in my mind, I couldn't stop. I wanted to stop. I played all kinds of tricks with myself to stop, and none of them worked." She pauses for a moment, collecting herself or her thoughts, and then continues. "I told you that I did some bad things. I'll tell you one. I didn't do anything bad with men; maybe that would have been better. I had some beautiful baskets and weavings my mother had brought over from Vietnam. I had an idea they were worth a lot of money. She had divided them between my brothers and sisters and me. She told us to keep them for our children and our children's children. She said they were our doorways to our past."

K-Siu closes her eyes for a moment. When she looks up, her eyes are filled with shame. "I sold all of mine. One by one. There are many Asian art dealers in Los Angeles. I found a man who did not ask questions. I could barely look at him when I took him the baskets. Each time, I said as little as I could. I felt so ashamed. My mother does not know. I think it would kill her if she did. I live every day with the fear that she will ask to see the baskets again. I miss her every day, but I am happy that she and my father live so far away."

Helen has been looking at the floor the whole time K-Siu has been speaking. "I sold my grandfather's watch," she nearly whispers. "He had brought it with him to Oklahoma when he pioneered. When I sold it, I didn't care. All I cared about was getting enough to go to the casino the next day—and keeping my husband from finding out what I was doing. I knew then."

"How can it be," K-Siu starts, "that I was terrified every minute I wasn't gambling—of what I was doing, of not having enough money to play again—and the fear didn't stop me? My mother told me stories of people in her village who had smoked Dragon Seed—opium. They were like that. Hungry ghosts, my people call them. I was a hungry ghost."

"I was a nightmare," Nora says. "I reached a point where I was trapped. I wasn't in denial anymore, but I still couldn't stop. I'd start out in the morning absolutely convinced it was the day I was done. I'd get through work, start to drive home, and then it was as if the truck had a mind of its own. Next thing I knew I'd be looking down at my watch and it would be almost midnight. I'd have to pee so bad I thought I'd explode. My blood sugar was in my toes. I was so dehydrated my heart was pounding, and I'd be staring at a computer screen, watching nothing but losses fall into place. One time I had a flash of clarity. I realized I'd become a woodworker because the last thing in the world I'd ever wanted was to become a computer nerd or a secretary—and there I was looking into a computer screen like it was the Holy Grail.

"More than once I snapped awake with my face resting against the slot machine. I'd finally max out the ATM and drag myself to the truck. I don't ever want to go back to what I felt sitting behind the steering wheel, looking out at the almost-empty parking lot and wondering if I'd have the guts to drive into a telephone pole on the way home."

"It was that bad for me, too," Helen says. "But it took me a while to catch on. Because I started out with bingo at the Veterans Hall, I felt that my gambling was just a little innocent fun—though I knew it was wrong to lie to my hubby even if I wanted to mercy-kill him most of the time. The mercy would have been for me. And I knew it was crazy to lie to my kids. I knew everybody else knew. I can't tell you the number of mornings I woke up at three, my brain rattling, and never went back to sleep. I hated that the most. I was scared they'd give me grief about what I was doing, and scared they wouldn't. My gambling girlfriends and I never said a word about how scared we were, except maybe for joking about being losers. We'd borrow money from each other and give each other tips on how to hide the credit cards from our husbands. Some of those girls are still out there. I don't envy them—and I do."

"I knew I was in trouble," I interject. "I tried to quit a dozen times." I tell the group about having been in a circle once before in Flagstaff and how I didn't last. "I started going because of how I would feel when I woke up in the casino hotel room after an all-nighter. I'd fall asleep about four in the morning and jolt awake at seven. My heart would pound so hard I'd think I was having a heart attack. My thoughts were piled on top of each other, each of them worse than the one above it, the whole stack threatening to crash at any time. But then would I get up, take a shower, put on my clothes, and leave?"

"Of course," Barb says, "and when you got home you'd look in the mirror, have a little talk with yourself, make out a nice budget, call the ever-so-sensible loan consolidation people, and make an honest woman of yourself."

There is a chorus of "Ha!"

"The *second* I was squared away at my slot machine with a cup of that free, puny casino coffee and two greasy donuts," I say, "and I slid a five into the money slot, I couldn't think what I'd been so freaked out about. Later, driving the two and a half hours home, the wake-up horror would come back to me. That was what got me to the first circle in Flagstaff. I stayed clean for maybe ten months, long enough to feel my brain clear. And then one day I was bored. The fuckits kicked in. I thought, *This time could be different,* and I was headed down the hill to the little Indian casino.

"I knew I'd crossed the line every time I gambled after that. I'm not even sure that this last time—the thing that got me here—made it finally sink in deep enough, either. If it hadn't been for those migraines, I bet I'd still be playing. I think my body itself wanted me to quit. It's always been smarter than my mind!"

"A few of my friends tried to talk to me," Barb says. "I shined them on. They were so naive about gambling addiction that it was easy. I now believe that a true compulsive gambler can't be talked, shamed, or threatened into quitting. It took getting busted for me to stop. Even now I want to understand more about this obsession. I've had gambling pals who quit cocaine tell me that playing slot machines is the closest thing to crack they can imagine—and they're still playing."

Candace proposes a break. I go out onto the back patio. I'm still raw from withdrawal, still facing each day that I won't ever be able to gamble with impunity again. I need to be alone with my thoughts, and with the stories we have just told each other. There is so much to learn, so much to take in, so much that invites me to face how much we are all alike. I am not the wild frontier outlaw woman I believed I was. I'm not Belle Starr heading out to the saloon for a heart-stopping night of poker in which I best all the boys.

I sit on the low wall that divides the patio from the raw desert. I think of the women I have met in the casinos, of the women in the Flagstaff Scheherazade's Sisters, of the women who write their stories for my friend Marilyn Lancelot's website, Women Helping Women. It doesn't matter how we started gambling or what we played. It doesn't matter how long it took for us to walk up to the line and suddenly find ourselves on the other side. Once the compulsion kicks in, all women gambling addicts are sisters.

I think of the signs and symptoms that tell most of us we are over the line: gambling till our last penny is gone, thinking constantly about gambling, lying to friends and family about our losses, losing interest in work and social connections, gambling money budgeted for necessities, using one or many credit card cash advances for gambling, and, for me, a binge gambler, the most telling indicator: only feeling normal when I am in the casino at my machine.

I knew the signs and symptoms, as did many of us who gamble compulsively, but perhaps the biggest symptom of all conned me into pretending that everything was just fine. Denial lay at the heart of my personal myopia about my actions. Denial may, in the long run, be as powerful a snare as the addiction itself.

Helen calls to me from the doorway. "It's almost time to start up again," she says. "Are you okay?"

"I am," I say. "I've been thinking about denial. Even now, the only way I cannot gamble is to do it a day at a time. If I think too far ahead, I think, *Maybe I could just. . . .* "

"Maybe," Helen says. "Oh yes. Maybe. That word goes through my head all the time. My daughter sent me the twenty questions that Gamblers Anonymous asks its new members. I answered 'yes' to fifteen of them. If you get seven, you're supposed to know you're in trouble. Guess what?"

"You thought it wasn't so bad?"

"Well," Helen laughs, "it wasn't all twenty."

Here are the GA Twenty Questions:

1. *Did you ever lose time from work or school due to gambling?*
2. *Has gambling ever made your home life unhappy?*
3. *Did gambling affect your reputation?*

4. Have you ever felt remorse after gambling?

5. Did you ever gamble to get money with which to pay debts or otherwise solve financial difficulties?

6. Did gambling cause a decrease in your ambition or efficiency?

7. After losing did you feel you must return as soon as possible and win back your losses?

8. After a win did you have a strong urge to return and win more?

9. Did you often gamble until your last dollar was gone?

10. Did you ever borrow to finance your gambling?

11. Have you ever sold anything to finance gambling?

12. Were you reluctant to use "gambling money" for normal expenditures?

13. Did gambling make you careless of the welfare of yourself or your family?

14. Did you ever gamble longer than you had planned?

15. Have you ever gambled to escape worry, trouble, boredom or loneliness?

16. Have you ever committed, or considered committing, an illegal act to finance gambling?

17. Did gambling cause you to have difficulty in sleeping?

18. Do arguments, disappointments or frustrations create within you an urge to gamble?

19. Did you ever have an urge to celebrate any good fortune by a few hours of gambling?

20. Have you ever considered self destruction or suicide as a result of your gambling?

GA teaches that most compulsive gamblers will answer yes to at least seven of these questions.

DOPAMINE IS QUEEN

GAMBLING AND THE BRAIN

Dopamine is Queen.
> —Steven C., in Howard Shaffer's *Expressions of Addiction*

The human brain lay cool and heavy in my gloved hands. I looked down on the brain's fragile and mysterious topography, the terrain of bulges and crevices. I imagined the unseen and intricate structures within. I wondered who had once occupied the mass of tissue and water, and in that instant I understood something about who I was. And wasn't.

It was 1972. I stood at a gray metal table in a neurophysiology laboratory. As a thirty-two-year-old graduate student in psychology, I had yet to encounter Sigmund Freud's patchwork of assumption and prejudice, Carl Jung's filigree of human emotion and behavior, Fritz Perls's gestalt mapping. It would be years before I would read New Age proponents' wishful notions that as we think, so we control our fate. I had studied with a student of B. F. Skinner's and come to believe that human behavior was nothing more than a complex of on-and-off responses to reward and punishment.

During my semester in the neurophysiology lab, I came to know the brain that I held that first day. I dissected it, made slides, listened to my professors, read, and asked questions. "My" brain, the brain I'd been assigned to study, weighed around 1,350 grams. It was composed of roughly 100 billion neurons, each of them a tiny transmitter of sensation, information, both outer signals and inner. There were glial cells—ten to fifty times as many of them as there were neurons. Their function was to surround neurons and hold them in place, to supply nutrients and oxygen, to insulate one neuron from another, to destroy pathogens and remove dead neurons, and to modulate neurotransmission.

If the "owner" of this brain had been a woman, she would have had 19.3 billion cortical cells. What she might have called her mind would have been made up of 77–78 percent water, 10–12 percent fats, 8 percent proteins, 1 percent carbohydrates, 2 percent soluble organic substances, and 1 percent organic salts. And, at any given moment, her "personality" would have been the product of the firing of myriads of the 0.15 quadrillion synapses in her cortex.

The more I learned, the more I understood that the mind was brain, and the brain was body. It all began with the physical structure. Everything else was stories we layered around that armature.

Later, as a private counselor and consultant, I often questioned why I had spent those grueling semesters studying the function of the brain. My mind does not move in a linear fashion. I can't simply memorize. If I don't know what meaning lies within a fact, I can't learn it. My professors were patient, but I suspect that they, too, wondered why a dreamer was intrigued by hard data.

I dabbled in Buddhism at that time, and the idea that who I thought I was and who you thought you were could be broken down into the mathematics of nerve cells and neurotransmitters seemed like knowledge that could lead to humility, and from there into the possibility of a little peace. But over the years, that knowledge seemed to have little bearing on the counseling work I did with my clients. It seemed coldly theoretical compared to the sweaty work of real healing and change.

So I subjected myself to the more technical classes, and yet, deep down I was uneasy with what I was learning. All the hard science seemed irrevocable, harsh, without room for magic or hope. If all we were was a complex of chemicals, membranes, and on-and-off signals, then what was the importance of human feelings, what was the point in believing in choices, accomplishments, failures, and disasters?

I tucked the knowledge of brain function away in my memory and went on to learn the theories of Freud, Jung, Carl Rogers, Fritz Perls. I discovered the beginnings of the feminist reconstruction of psychology and moved on to things that captured my fascination and my heart.

I'm eight months into not gambling by the time the Scheherazade's Sisters have told all our stories. I drive home that night thinking about the connections between our stories and the brain science I had learned over thirty years earlier.

The highway up to the mesa upon which my little cabin stands is blessedly free of other cars. Stars and a quarter moon float above me. Joshua trees are skeletal against the horizon. In the solitude and delicate light, I find my thoughts slowing down. Memories drift up.

We Sisters have spent many of these past weeks talking about our families. Most of us were raised in families where one or both parents were gamblers or alcoholics or suffered from a serious mental disorder. As each woman spoke, I kept thinking about an article I'd recently read about genetics and gambling addiction. I felt as though it held the answer to a question I had carried since my graduate years.

As I pull into my driveway, it suddenly occurs to me why I had been drawn to study the brain. The intensity of my own obsession with gambling has never been so fully revealed as it has over these weeks of personal sharing with the Sisters. I suspect that the knowledge I'd gained all those years ago may have stayed dormant until I needed it. I park, go to the single lawn chair in my front yard, and sit for a while under the huge, silent sky. I need to let the thoughts swirling in my mind settle out—and the feelings.

How could it have been that I had once learned about the exquisite and easily disrupted balance within our skulls and still taken my own delicate brain into obsessive interaction with slot machines? I am frightened by how close I have come to permanently destroying my mind. And I know that with a turn of the ignition and a short drive to a nearby casino, I could be on my way to annihilation again.

In fourteen years of compulsive gambling, and a few years' time with the Flagstaff women's circle and Scheherazade's Sisters, I have learned that I will never be able to gamble normally again. Something has altered in my brain. I suddenly want to learn more about what has taken me captive.

This quiet moment on the desert mesa, from which there is no place left to run, finally allows me to face the impact that my addiction has had on my brain, a brain that is not a construct, but a physical organ. I finally feel ready to explore the deeper underpinnings of my own obsession.

The air cools. I go inside, greet the four cats, and log on to my computer to reread the paper I found a few days ago. It is Dr. David Comings's work with genetics and gambling addiction. As I read, I'm grateful for my psychology teachers' patient efforts thirty years ago to teach linear information to a wild mind. Comings wrote about a genetic inability in some people to fully utilize dopamine, the neurotransmitter implicated in a vast array of human thinking, feeling, and behavior.

The news is both hard to take and welcome. I suspect I am one of those with the genetic defect. There are long histories of depression, bipolar disorder, and compulsion on both sides of my family. Knowledge is the link between the realities of my brain and the possibility of recovery. Without knowing the intricate workings of human physiology and genetics as the foundation for understanding human addiction, there's little possibility of addressing the roots of addiction and evolving effective treatment strategies.

I'm hooked. I surf through dozens of articles on dopamine. One leads to another to another to even more. Of course, as a compulsive woman, I have to force myself to stop—but at least I'm not sliding bills into a machine. By the time I finally go to bed at two in the morning, I know a lot more about why the women in my circle and I have been so thoroughly enthralled by an activity we had each suspected—or known—was killing us.

I decide to create a handout for the Sisters about our brains and take it to the next meeting.

QUEEN DOPAMINE

Every part of the brain contains nerve cells and neurotransmitters. Nerve cells, also called neurons, are the basic cells of the nervous system. They are found in the brain and spinal cord, and in peripheral nerves throughout the body. They have an irregular "body," which contains the nucleus of the cell. One long, threadlike axon and smaller, branching dendrites project from the central body of the cell. The neurons release and receive neurotransmitters.

Nerve cells communicate with one another and with other cells by exchanging neurotransmitters. Neurotransmitters are physiological chemicals that carry, amplify, and modulate signals in many other cells in addition to neurons. They cross the space between the neuron that's sending a transmission and the neuron that's receiving the transmission. The space is called the synaptic cleft.

While many neurotransmitters play a part in how we think, how we feel, and how we move and experience, there's one neurotransmitter in particular that plays the biggest role in the establishment and maintenance of addictions: dopamine. A simple and accurate description of how dopamine functions in addictions can be found on the MedHelp website. It was written by an anonymous recovering crack addict, a sister to those of us who gamble. Here are her words:

Brain chemicals, including dopamine, are stored in cells, which you can think of like barrels full of that chemical. When something occurs like a good meal or great sex the brain pours out some dopamine from the dopamine barrels into an open space in the brain called a synapse. It floats around there. Think of the synapse like a street, and dopamine is like little cars driving around aimlessly on the street.

Across the street (not far) from the barrels of dopamine are dopamine receptors. These receptors have little parking spaces on them that only fit dopamine (or a substance VERY similar in chemical shape to dopamine) into them, like a lock and key. As the dopamine floats around in the synapse, it finds parking spaces at dopamine receptors, and "plugs in" to the receptors. THIS is the point where we feel good, when the dopamine is parked in a receptor's parking space. There are, however, a limited number of receptors with "dopamine only parking" available, and each receptor has a limited number of parking spaces. So some of the dopamine may not be able to find a place to park.

When all the parking spaces are taken, the remaining dopamine that didn't find a place to park is normally recycled. There are "reuptake molecules" that do this—think of them like tow trucks. They find the extra dopamine, and tow it back to the barrels of dopamine so that it can be re-used the next time. After some time has passed, the receptors release the dopamine that was parked in their parking spaces, and the tow trucks take those dopamine molecules back to the barrel too.

The brain has a safety-check system that will destroy any excess dopamine that isn't in a parking space, and didn't get picked up by the tow truck. There are special chemicals in our brains that will break down this extra dopamine. Think of this like the toxic waste crew coming in and sweeping up the street.

As a last resort, after repeated long-term over-stimulation, the brain will shut down dopamine receptors so that nothing can park there ever again. Think of this like the demolition team coming in and permanently barricading off the driveways.

It is no accident that a recovering crack addict writes about dopamine. Dr. Hans Breiter, primary researcher at Massachusetts General Hospital, mapped the area of the brain that "lights up" in the presence of a gambling win. It is identical to the area that lights up when a person does cocaine.

Dopamine is a phenethylamine—a chemical found in trace amounts in chocolate, not an insignificant fact for women! Dopamine activates five types of dopamine receptors—D1, D2, D3, D4, and D5. The D2 receptor is the one that's altered in those of us with the genetic defect in dopamine utilization—our brains don't use dopamine as efficiently as others' brains do.

The pattern of dopamine release and utilization in the brain of a predisposed person who is gambling may initially be the normal fluctuations of a nonusing brain. But for the woman who carries the gene that alters her ability to utilize dopamine or has other predisposing factors, such as dysfunctional family history or inherited psychological disorders, those normal fluctuations can shift quickly into exaggerated highs and lows *without* injecting, ingesting, or inhaling a thing. Contemporary research has discovered that visual cues and patterns of reward delivery have as powerful an effect on dopamine responses as drugs do. Slot machines are deliberately programmed to take advantage of the brain's dopamine responses to visual cues and patterns of "hits" and jackpots. In fact, veteran gamblers, gambling treatment professionals, and gambling industry workers often call slot machines the crack cocaine of gambling.

Dopamine and other neurotransmitters are constantly circulating and recirculating through the normal brain in a natural ebb and flow. But in the addict's brain, dopamine levels occur as riptides, flash floods, and near-killing droughts. Since dopamine's many functions include the regulation of behavior and cognition, motor activity, motivation and reward, sleep, mood, attention, and learning, you can guess what those flash floods and droughts do to us.

Basically, when an addict uses, dopamine surges way beyond normal limits, resulting in the normal dopamine stores being depleted—again and again. When the addict is in withdrawal, many of the harsh symptoms can be traced to that depleted dopamine system. While the other neurotransmitters are part of the action, dopamine is believed to be the primary chemical responsible for the highs and the lows.

During that long night of research, I came across an Internet posting by Dr. Howard Shaffer, a prominent figure at Harvard Medical School in both the research and the treatment of gambling addiction, who created a powerful photographic exhibit called *Expressions of Addiction*. I was struck by how one of his subjects, Steven C., a polyaddicted user, summed up dopamine. He told the doctor, "Dopamine is Queen!"

So what's the impact on me and my dopamine-challenged cohorts? We may operate with some degree (mild to severe) of anhedonia, a psychological condition characterized by an inability to experience pleasure in normally pleasurable acts. For me this manifests itself in having a brain always one bet away from normal. Many gambling addicts say that the only time they feel normal is when they are in action.

Dopamine is also the chemical from which the neurotransmitter norepinephrine is made. Norepinephrine affects parts of the brain where attention and responding actions are controlled. It also jazzes up heart rate and glucose release. It can get you high and make you jittery and anxious.

Dopamine is a big player in helping us sleep, but it also does so much more. It was once believed that dopamine's primary role in the brain was in the experience of pleasure, but new research reveals a more complex picture.

Scientists now believe that dopamine has an essential role in determining why we pay attention to what we see, hear, smell, taste, and touch. Even more critical for the gambling addict, dopamine impacts our ability to perceive and guess at the delivery of a reward—and to get high off that process. Unexpected positive reward triggers the strongest surge of dopamine in the brain. It is easy to imagine how those of us with the genetic inability to utilize dopamine begin to seek those surges.

Unpleasant experiences, like physical pain or being startled, also cause surges in dopamine. In fact, dopamine rises in response to many triggers: drugs and alcohol; food (for the food addict or no food for the anorexic); romantic infatuation; video-gaming; self-mutilation; risk-taking (extreme sports, playing the stock market, business ventures); and compulsive working and controlling others (much of this is manifested in the perfectionism that leads to the Great American Addiction—busyness). Addicts always know what "fixes" their brains.

For the woman compulsive gambler who knows she must stop, the hard truth is that even thinking about a "fix" can trigger dopamine surges. Both anticipating and recalling gambling wins (including subliminal images associated with gambling) can get the addict high. And that anticipation and recall doesn't have to be based on a win. Thoughts of a favorite casino, of the moment of walking in through the doors with a pocket full of cash and a head full of hope, of the relief that fills the compulsive gambler at the instant of the first bet—all of these produce a dopamine rush.

It's logical to assume that many gambling addicts come to the obsession with other predispositions. There is a dopamine dysfunction in many mental, emotional, and behavioral disorders, including schizophrenia, depression (bipolar, unipolar, and atypical), attention deficit disorder, obsessive-compulsive disorder, and many impulse control disorders. Some compulsive gamblers may have an underlying dopamine dysfunction long before they set foot in a casino, log on to an online gambling site, engage in stock market play, buy a lottery ticket, or sit down to a friendly game of cards or Bunco.

If a woman wants to speed up the ride into the inevitable fun house nightmare, she can multitask her addictions, shoving twenties into the slot machine, gulping "free" margaritas, smoking cigarettes, and checking her cell phone every fifteen minutes to see if "he" has called.

The harshest fact in all of this is this: In the addicted brain, using ultimately depletes dopamine.

To keep it simple, sisters, here's a list of those dopamine facts:

1. Some people are born with a genetic inability to fully utilize dopamine. It's more complicated than a diabetic's inability to use insulin, but similar. The D2 receptor in an addict is different than in a "normal" person.

2. Dopamine is linked with pleasure.

3. Those with a genetic inability to utilize dopamine may operate with some degree (mild to severe) of anhedonia, a psychological condition characterized by an inability to experience pleasure in normally pleasurable acts.

4. Unexpected positive reward triggers the strongest surge of dopamine in the brain.

5. Genetically dopamine-impaired people may begin to seek those surges. (Cruel paradox: Once one begins to seek that surge, the positive reward is no longer unexpected. Bring on the slot machines with their variable reinforcement ratios.)

6. Unpleasant experiences—like physical pain or being startled— also cause surges in dopamine.

7. Dopamine rises in response to many other triggers as well, including:
   - drugs and alcohol
   - food
   - romantic infatuation
   - gambling
   - video-gaming
   - self-mutilation
   - risk-taking
   - anticipation of reward
   - recall of reward
   - romance or big money fantasizing

   The triggers seems nearly infinite: compulsive working, manipulating others, busyness

8. There is a dopamine dysfunction in many mental, emotional, and behavioral disorders, including schizophrenia, depression, attention deficit disorder, obsessive-compulsive disorder, and many impulse control disorders.

9. If you want to speed up the ride into the fun house, go for polyaddiction.

10. In D2-impaired brains, using ultimately depletes dopamine.

THE SISTERS CHECK IN

I go to the next meeting of Scheherazade's Sisters armed with my handouts and the intention to share what I am learning. That night, a new woman joins our circle. Ginny walks in primly, sits in a straight-back chair, and bursts into tears. She is a wire-thin African American woman with a drawn face.

We begin our usual round of introductions—each woman gives her name and tells about one gift the previous week has given her. Ginny watches each of us speak. We've all been in her place. We know she is measuring the time she has left before it's her turn, the time in which, if need be, she can get up and leave without saying a word—and go back to a deadly hobby.

Candace is sitting to her right, and when she finishes speaking, Ginny takes a deep breath. "I'm Ginny, and I can't think of one good thing about last week. Not one. I cannot believe I'm here. My mom and dad gambled till there was nothing left. I was always home taking care of my brothers and sisters. When I was fifteen, I promised myself I would never, ever set foot in a casino. I don't smoke or drink. I'm happily married, and I'm a great mom. I'm here because I was driving back from the casino, wondering what would happen if I crashed my car into the median."

She shrugs and nods to Delfina, who's sitting to her left. "Your turn," she says.

Delfina turns to face Ginny. "I'm glad you're here. There are a few of us who have wanted to kill ourselves because of this addiction. It's a miracle to me that a few days this last week were actually fun."

When it's my turn, I tell the group about my research. "What Ginny just told us fits completely with what I'm learning about brain chemistry and gambling. I brought some handouts."

Before I can even reach for them, Candace shouts out, "Give me one! All I've wanted to do this whole week is to top off the gas in the car, cash out my savings account, and head for the casino. I don't even know why. If what you're learning can help me sit on my damn hands—except maybe to pick up a phone and call one of you—I want to know all of it."

"First of all," I say, "the handout is titled 'Queen Dopamine' because I read a great quote from someone online who referred to dopamine this way—and it so captures the role dopamine plays in the lives of addicts."

We take a few minutes to read the handouts. Sharon looks up and grins. "That's right about gambling and coke. My husband and I fooled around with coke when we were younger. The rush I get—I mean got—from a really big jackpot is the same rush I used to get from cocaine."

"What about other kinds of speed?" Barb asks. "You know, crack, meth? One time when I actually was gracious enough to talk to the person at the machine next to me, I found out she was a tweaker on a hitting streak. She kept saying, 'Oh yeah, baby. Oh yeah. I've met you before.' When I asked her what she meant, she leaned over and whispered in my ear, 'This is meth, crack, and freebasing cocaine all rolled into one.'"

"She was right," I say. "A lot of that is what I want to share with you—it's there in the handout."

"Why, here's a brain!" Candace laughs and points. "I used to have one of those."

We talk for a while and then take a break. All the Sisters are staring at their handouts. The fact that they're so absorbed in the material is gratifying. I imagine a lot of them—or all of them—are having the same "Aha!" moment I had the night of the last meeting, under the desert sky in front of my little cabin.

Barb laughs, "I've got to say that I can't remember the last time I had a good, sparkly romantic infatuation. Maybe if I had had sex now and then, say once every two years, gambling wouldn't have been such a big deal. But after my last lover booked, forget about it. And the casino was only ten minutes away."

"Oh yeah," Candace says, "how many times have I caught myself patting my machine and saying, "'Come on, sugar. Haven't I been good to you? Now give it up'?"

"Yeah," I say, "dopamine rules."

We settle back into our circle.

Nora waves the handout at us. "This is way scary stuff," she says. "I'm not just intellectually overwhelmed. I think this is the first time I've really understood how truly powerless I am over gambling. And why it might take so long to get some normal feelings back once we quit."

"I was pretty blindsided by what I found," I say. "I don't understand why more of this information isn't going out to the general public. Learning about dopamine killed off any illusions I might have been harboring about being able to gamble normally someday."

Ginny raises her hand. "Delfina asked me if I'd tell more of my story. That almost made me want to bail, but then I figured I could use some of the information on this handout to catch you up on who I've been. It'll make it easier for me. I still feel pretty shaky."

"Whatever works," Nora says. "That's the only rule here."

"That genetic stuff really fits me," Ginny starts. "'Those with a genetic inability to utilize dopamine may operate with some degree of anhedonia . . .'" she reads aloud.

"I've *never* been a very happy person. I just figured it was because of how I dealt with the craziness in my childhood. I was the oldest and ended up taking care of the other kids. There wasn't any money, so we five kids were in a one-bedroom apartment. When bedtime came, I was too exhausted to sleep, so I would take a blanket into the bathtub, turn on the bathroom light, curl up, and read.

"When I look back, it seems as though I was numb clear up till the first time I walked into a casino. A couple of my friends wanted to see a show. I never made it to the show. I sat down at the first slot machine I saw—just to see what the big deal was, made a couple twenty-line, nickel-a-line bets, and that was it. For the first time in my life, I was having fun."

Helen nods. "A lot of us never started out to gamble, but we went with friends, tried it once, and that was all she wrote. You listen to our stories and you'll hear you're not the only middle-aged little girl in the world!"

"I felt like a kid when I hit on my second bet," Ginny says, "a $500 jackpot on a 45¢ bet. I felt like I'd eaten a pound of really good chocolate!" She laughs for the first time. "I wanted more. And more and more."

Candace points to the handout and reads aloud again. "'Unexpected positive reward triggers the strongest surge of dopamine in the brain. Genetically dopamine-impaired people may begin to seek those surges.'"

"Yeah," Nora says, "you gotta see how a slot machine is the perfect drug for a gambling addict—I can't tell you how often I'd start to get bored when the machine was chilly, and I'd go like, 'Whoa, wake up, girl, any second something fabulous could happen. You just don't know!' A big hit was *always* unexpected."

"And then," Ginny says, "it's Catch-22, because once you get hooked the reward is no longer a big surprise, except on a slot machine because that must be how they're programmed."

"Exactly," Sharon cuts in, "the payout systems are designed to keep you expecting the unexpected. I recently read an article in *The New York Times* about this. These computer nerds know how to program slots to fit what might hook all different kinds of players."

We all go quiet. Nora shakes her head.

"I've got to keep talking while I've got my nerve up," Ginny says. "This is weird, but it all makes sense to me, even the part about bad experiences jacking up dopamine. I remember getting a buzz from worrying about how I would pay the bills. It was as though the worrying filled an empty space in my thoughts that I have always been afraid of—or," she stops and looks up at me, "maybe that's about the adrenaline you were talking about."

"Hey," I say, "as far as I'm concerned, anything is better than normal—normal is like flatline to me."

"The information on underlying psychological problems," Ginny says, "makes me wonder about who I am under the addiction. I've always been a workaholic. I figured it's because I'm African American, and no matter how far we come, most of us sisters still believe we have to try harder. But reading this makes me wonder. Because once I quit, something really scary started to happen."

"You're driving yourself nuts obsessing about everything?" Sharon asks.

"Yes! I keep thinking about that old lyric about dropping in to see what condition your condition is in. I am so bored of thinking about my thinking!"

Delfina shakes her head. "You know, I learned psychology theory when I got my social work degree, and they give us in-service trainings at the rehab center I work at, but this brain stuff is bottom-line. You can fight the system, but you can't fight your own brain."

We close the circle and clean up. I drive home with a busy brain. I can't stop thinking about the hard, hard work of stopping an addiction. I'm struck by how Ginny's face softened as we all talked. I am moved by how much the stories of the other sisters mirrored parts of hers—and mine.

I need to talk more. I call Sharon, and I'm grateful when she answers.

"I can't stop thinking," I say.

She laughs. "Honey, you are the most obsessive-compulsive of the obsessive-compulsive. Women like us never stop thinking. That lies under our addictions for a lot of us—and that's part of how you write. What's up?"

"It's frightening to me that my brain isn't normal."

There is a moment of silence. "I'm thinking," she says after a moment. "Or maybe I'm feeling. Hard to tell with me. I know what you mean, though, and it pisses me off to not be able to just do whatever I want to do—and as much of it as I want to do. But I know I'm not alone. The diabetic, my bipolar brother, the epileptic, the schizophrenic—we're all walking that same path."

"Thanks for the pep talk," I say.

"Back atcha," Sharon says. I can see the tough-chick grin on her face. "At least we have each other."

FREUD WAS WRONG

PSYCHODYNAMICS OF GAMBLING ADDICTION

The god Krishna says, "I am the game of the gambler."
—The Bhagavad Gita, ancient Hindu scripture

Everett, my best friend, road trip pal, and gambling buddy, and I climbed up to an alcove in the Leppy Hills, a low mountain range a little north of Wendover, Nevada. It was 2004, and we were taking a break from the Rainbow, our favorite Wendover casino. He liked the joint because it still had old-fashioned three-reel nickel slot machines on which he could prolong his TOD—time on device in gambling industry terms—by playing his famous Everett system: one nickel, then two nickels, then three nickels, then four, then five, *unless* he gets a win, after which he plays five. He knew I thought he was nuts. The famous Everett system was far too slow for me. I liked the Rainbow Casino because they had half a dozen Cleopatra nine-line machines—and the all-you-can-eat spaghetti, meatballs, and garlic bread special.

Everett and I were taking a break from the casino because hiking and climbing in the desert is one of the few things we love as much as gambling, and we were taking a break because he was down 50 bucks and I was down 200.

"We're ancient," I said. Everett pulled out his flat wallet and said, "I sure feel ancient."

"That's not what I mean," I said, "I read about this area. They found bone gambling pieces in the ancient caves here. These people were betting on rabbit skins around ten thousand years ago."

Ev laughed. "When you get obsessed, you really get obsessed. Speaking of obsession, the sun's about to blast this alcove; we better get back to the climate-controlled temperature of the Rainbow."

We climbed down, drove back, and walked into the cool casino gloom. It felt like we'd entered a shady and sheltering cave. The twenty-four-hour spaghetti special called to me. We fueled up. We were wiping the last of the spaghetti sauce up with garlic bread when Ev said, "Let's go win some rabbit skins." We paid up, tipped lavishly, and headed back to our digital gambling bones.

Humans have gambled as long as they have had opposable thumbs—for far longer than they have had theories about why Og could toss down the bone dice for an hour and walk away while Snarg bet against anybody who would play till all her rabbit skins were gone. Gambling pieces and stories have been found everywhere our human ancestors lived. The original people of America gambled long before the European invasion began.

The Assiniboin of North Dakota used two-sided dice made from pottery shards or crow claws—one side black, the other red—and it is legend that Assiniboin men would beat their wives who lost too much at gambling. Pawnee men might have been slightly more philosophical about their wives' obsession; one of their old sayings has an almost plaintive note: "Hungry is the man whose wife gambles." Many of the early Pueblo people of the Southwest bet on foot races. The Navajo still love the Shoe Game, only played in winter and involving teams of "Day Animals" and "Night Animals." One player hides a yucca ball in a shoe. The other team has to guess in which shoe the ball is hidden. One side sings songs as the opposing team tries to find the ball. The Day Animal and Night Animal songs have been passed down through generations.

The European invasion brought more gambling. Voyageurs and mountain men and prospectors relieved the boredom of long winter nights shooting dice and playing poker. The Chinese workers imported for near-slave labor in Western mines and on the railroads brought Pak Kop Piu, the traditional game that evolved into keno.

Charles Frey invented the first mechanical slot machine in 1895 and, in 1901, designed and made the first mechanical draw poker machine. The first all-electronic gambling machine was built by Nevada Electronic in 1964. The Fortune Coin Company built the first electronic slot machine in 1975. And beginning in the late 1930s with Nevada, casinos became legal across most of the States.

Fyodor Dostoyevsky wrote perhaps the most accurate and poignant account of compulsive gambling in his 1867 novel, *The*

Gambler. Not only does the hero, Alexei, gamble himself into ruin, but his grandmother loses almost 100,000 rubles in one session at the roulette table. Dostoyevsky, too, suffered from a severe gambling compulsion. It is thought that he wrote his best-known novel, *Crime and Punishment*, at top speed to earn the advance to pay his gambling debts.

Dostoyevsky's addiction became the subject of the first psychological conjecture about what caused compulsive gambling. Though Karl Marx aligned gambling with religion as an opiate of the masses, and some mid-nineteenth-century social scientists hypothesized that compulsive gambling was a way to deal with the pressures and unfair demands of industrialization, the Viennese father of modern psychology, Sigmund Freud, had a wildly different take. He believed that Dostoyevsky gambled compulsively to punish himself for his early childhood sexual longings for his mother. His theory continued to carry weight for decades, with students and followers applying elaborate variations on this theme to gambling addicts in general.

Ralph Greenson went along with the mental masturbation kick but also theorized that there were three different kinds of gamblers. The normal gambler plays for fun and can stop anytime. The professional gambler gambles for a living, mostly card games or sports betting. The neurotic gambler can't stop and is completely run by the need to gamble.

Freud's most renowned student, Carl Jung, rarely referred directly to the gambler, but his theories of the human psyche hold implications for those of us snared in compulsion. One of his clients wrote in his dream journal, "Awake my soul, stretch every nerve. I am the Game of the Gambler." Jung, who was fascinated by symbols and metaphor, connected his client's words to certain Eastern teachings, in which radiance and gods were present in the gambler's dice. For Jung, the elements of weather and fire, the instinctual natures of wild creatures, and the unpredictable and uncontrollable fall of the dice were all part of a same passionate and wondrous chaos.

For Jung, the human mind and spirit were inseparable, and he understood the way certain images and sounds can play on human minds and spirits. If he were alive today, he might see the whirling Cleopatras and ankhs and lotuses of the modern Queen of the Nile slot machine as the components of a meditation mandala. He might hear the buzzers and bells as trance-inducing cues for the child in our unconscious minds.

Jung is also known for his theory of archetypes. He believed that each of us contains a constellation (some would call it a committee) of individual "personalities." He went beyond Freud's notion of the id, the ego, and the superego—the chaotic child, the adult, and the overarching conscience or controller. For Jung, we contained within us goddesses, beggars, kings, prostitutes, infant and adult, man and woman, profane and sacred.

These archetypes do not classify a person. Instead, each of us contains all of the basic ones: shadow, anima, animus, and self. The shadow is a mirror of the deeper—often maligned—elements of our psyche. It may also be a part of ourselves we have denied. The shadow hates rules. It loves what is exotic and forbidden. It will sometimes reveal itself to us in dreams, both night and day. It can take over when we are uncertain or drugged out. And it can certainly sport the slouched hat and green eyeshades of the gambling man, or the fanny pack and sensible shoes of the stereotyped slot queen granny.

The shadow is a creature of fascination. Jung believed that we needed to pay attention to our fascinations, obsessions, and fixations, or else we might be fooled by our stories that we are either paragons of virtue or monsters of depravity. He knew, too, that we meet in every person and every situation we encounter pieces of ourselves, and knowing as much as we can about ourselves allows us to live with integrity.

The anima is the unconscious feminine aspect of the male. The animus is the unconscious masculine aspect of the woman. And then there is an array of other Jungian lesser archetypes. The trickster may be accompanying the compulsive woman gambler stepping through the doors of a casino or logging on to gamble; the magician or the sorceress might beguile her; the nurturing, soothing mother might seem to cradle her in the foggy bliss of the zone.

Jung believed that the self was a meld of the physical being and the higher power. It is part of and connects with the greater universe. He would have found the work of contemporary therapy, healing, and/or recovery to be the restoration of wholeness in the addict.

In January 1961, Carl Jung wrote a letter to Bill W., the co-founder of Alcoholics Anonymous. He was responding to a query from Bill about one of his clients, Roland H. Jung conjectured that Roland H. was suffering not so much from a thirst for alcohol as a thirst for spiritual meaning. He suggested that the only real way to "quench" the thirst for alcohol might be to set out on a path of spiritual seeking. He pointed out that *spiritus* means both alcohol and the heights of spiritual awareness. Jung understood that for some it was necessary to turn to spiritual help—what the twelve-step programs call a higher power.

Billye B. Currie, a licensed psychologist and graduate of the Inter-Regional Society of Jungian Analysts, writes in her book, *The Gambler*, "My interest in the gambler is quite personal and filled with emotional intensity. There is the gut-wrenching sadness when my ten-year-old client tells of mom's descent into the depths of gambling pathology—the end of the family, as she knew it, and the beginning of the monster dreams that strike fear in her."

Currie goes on to apply Jungian principles and analysis to the compulsive gambler. She writes eloquently about how archetypes unexamined can lead to impulses, how a deep split between the dark side and the light side within can leave the gambler trapped in guilt—a guilt that can only be soothed by more gambling, the deep natural longing for *spiritus*, the condition of exaltation that addicts call being high.

Currie, like Jung, understands the powerful hypnotic effect of certain symbols—meditation mandalas in Eastern religion, sacred icons that move the complex of archetypes, the power of chanting and repetition to induce trance.

I love to imagine Currie and Jung, one living, the other dead, walking into a modern casino. They would see the brilliantly colored slot machines, study the repeating patterns in the carpets under their feet, hear the incantatory repetitions of the bells and buzzer, and see the elements of a gaudy and somewhat sinister temple. Currie and her ghostly mentor would look at the fascinated players—at the whirling roulette wheel; at the red, black, and green quilt of the dice tables; at the glowing machines. They would see the devotion, and they would neither judge nor condemn the worshippers; they would only feel empathy.

On the other hand, if the late psychologist B. F. Skinner were to see today's insidiously designed electronic slot machines, he would find nothing cosmic or mysterious in their workings—though he, too, would not judge the gambling addicts. B. F. Skinner was the Edgar Pierce Professor of Psychology at Harvard University from 1958 until his retirement in 1974, and, through meticulous experimentation and observation, the founder of the experimental analysis of behavior, a branch of behaviorism.

Behaviorism keeps it simple. An animal (humans are biologically animals) that is rewarded for a behavior will repeat the behavior. An animal that is punished for a behavior will cease the behavior. Skinner went beyond that basic model to define "schedules of reinforcement," the consequences of particular patterns of reinforcement.

Schedules of reinforcement, both positive and negative, are dependent on interval (fixed or variable) and ratio (fixed or variable). Skinner developed three schedules of reinforcement: continuous reinforcement; interval (fixed/variable) reinforcement; and ratio (fixed or variable) reinforcement.

Continuous positive reinforcement means that the subjects performing a behavior get a reward every single time they make the behavior. Long before Skinner and his elegantly calibrated data-recording instruments, wise old wives' tales taught that too much of a good thing inevitably leads to satiation and disinterest. Skinner observed the same phenomenon in his experimental subjects.

Continuous punishment (negative reinforcement) eventually brings about cessation of the behavior—though watching a compulsive gambler on a cold slot machine or at a cold blackjack table would seem to contradict that experimental finding. In fact, it is the power of intermittent positive and negative reinforcement that keeps the unlucky player gambling.

Gambling operates on variable interval and ratio reinforcement. Variable is the operative definer. Not knowing when the positive reinforcement will be delivered and hoping the negative reinforcement is just a run of bad luck may be the only behavioral hook a compulsive gambler needs to keep playing. Intermittent positive reinforcement is the most powerful way to train and sustain a behavior. Slot machine designers know this. The computer geniuses who program today's slot machine payout delivery systems are wizards of behavioral psychology and neurochemistry.

The brain chemistry flash floods and droughts that respond to the cannily programmed slot machine systems are not based solely on financial reward. While most action players (card, roulette, dice, sports betters) seem to be hooked by the rush of the "action," slot players seek being in the zone, a mental state of both anticipation and numbness. It is common to hear slot machine addicts say that all a win means to them is more playing time. Yet again, random positive reinforcement and dopamine rule.

It is of particular significance for the compulsive gambler that Skinner's reinforcement theories apply not only to physical actions but also to thoughts. That knowledge can lead to making changes both in how gamblers behave and in how they think. Obsessive or impulsive thinking is almost always the precursor to gambling. And recurring intrusive thoughts of gambling fun—called euphoric recall—are powerful triggers for destruction.

British researcher Dr. Mark Griffiths at Nottingham Trent University and his Australian colleague Dr. Paul Delfabbro at the University of Adelaide applied the principles of Skinner's operant conditioning to an understanding of the addictive gambling process. The slot machine's random delivery of reward is powerful, but the fact that the player can make bets rapidly (more rapidly, I would add, than in any other form of gambling) is even more insidious. I once kept track of my own frequency of bets: seventeen bets a minute—and during my most compulsive phase of gambling, each bet was anywhere from $1 to $5.

A relatively new version of behaviorism, rational emotive behavior therapy (REBT), teaches clients to manage their thoughts and actions. REBT is a cognitive-behavioral approach for treatment of stress, depression, hostility, and anxiety developed by Dr. Albert Ellis in 1955.

According to REBT theorists, emotional and behavioral ailments are the result of irrational thoughts, assumptions, and beliefs. This therapy identifies those problematic and erroneous ideas and replaces them with more rational, reality-based thoughts and perspectives.

The process of identifying gambling trigger thoughts and replacing them can slow down the hair-trigger decisions of the gambling addict who is also afflicted with impulse control disorder. Impulse control disorder can be loosely defined by a person's failure to resist an un-thought-out act or behavior that may be harmful to self or others. Once the thought pops up, the action follows almost instantly.

Most of us in Scheherazade's Sisters have talked about the almost-alchemical shift in our thinking when the urge to gamble strikes. I remember being engaged in writing or reading and suddenly thinking, *What the hell? I'm going!* and racing to grab my wallet, water bottle, slot machine card—and I was out the door. Once the thought had triggered the behavior, there was never any turning back. I cannot remember a single time when I thought with equal suddenness, *This is crazy,* and turned the car toward home—and that includes times when there were only $40 in my pocket and $25 in my savings account that would keep my account viable.

My impulsivity extends to almost every area of my life. I grab the marionberry pie off the shelf at Trader Joe's knowing full well that I battle late-onset diabetes on a daily basis. I fire off an email to potential male Trouble. And I also stop, sit on a rock wall in the middle of a long hike, pull out my journal, and write something like *smudged silver moon, pink clouds, an osprey guarding its chicks*. The worst in my life and the best in my life are often the direct results of an irresistible impulse.

Given that dopamine levels surge in the addicted brain at even the thought of a fix, it makes sense to me that even the thought gets me high. Consequently, I am thinking with an intoxicated brain even before I indulge in the intoxicant.

Gambling addiction experts point to comorbidity as a factor in the establishment of gambling addiction. Comorbidity means that compulsive gamblers come to gambling with a predisposition to depression, bipolar disorder, personality disorders, obsessive-compulsive disorder (OCD), and/or other issues. Since dopamine figures into all of these nervous system dysfunctions, it's reasonable to assume that compulsive gamblers are medicating their brain with gambling. Compulsive gambling, like compulsive shopping, stock market investing, and borrowing money, is often a component of a manic episode.

In addition, many compulsive gamblers are coaddicted—alcohol, drugs, food, cigarettes, speed, painkillers, sugar—anything to bring about an altered state of consciousness. I spent years engaged in yo-yo dieting, in on-and-off recovery for romance addiction and codependency, and forcing myself to take breaks from my work addiction. Anything I like, I want more of—until more becomes a means to annihilation.

Dr. Alex Blaszczynski and Lia Nower in the Department of Psychology at the University of Sydney, Australia, published an elegant and illuminating paper in 2001 about problem and pathological gambling. Blaszczynski and Nower propose that there are three basic types of compulsive gamblers, which they describe here in their analysis of Pathway 1, 2, and 3 gamblers:

[A] proportion of gamblers are essentially "normal" in character; that is, they do not show signs of premorbid psychological disturbance but simply lose control over gambling in response to the effects of conditioning and distorted cognitions surrounding probability of winning. Their "pathological gambling" is a transient state where fluctuations between heavy and excessive gambling are observed, a condition which also may remit spontaneously or with minimal interventions.

Pathway 1 gamblers may achieve sustained controlled gambling post-intervention.

. . . [A] second subgroup [Pathway 2 gamblers] is characterized by disturbed family and personal histories, poor coping and problem-solving skills, affective instability due to both biological and psychosocial deficits and later onset of gambling. Gambling is pursued as a means of emotional escape through dissociation or a medium aimed at regulating negative mood states or physiological states of hyper- or hypo-arousal.

The third group [Pathway 3 gamblers] in this schema is characterized by a biological vulnerability toward impulsivity, early onset, attentional deficits, antisocial traits and poor response to treatment. Dysfunctional neurological structures and functions and dysregulation of neurotransmitter systems underpin this vulnerability.

From a clinical perspective, each pathway contains different implications for choice of management strategies and treatment interventions. Clinical observations supported by empirical data suggest that Pathway 3 gamblers are typified by an antisocial impulsivist personality dimension manifesting a wide range of multiple dysfunctional behaviour including substance abuse, criminal offences and social instability.

These clinical features correlate with early onset gambling, more severe gambling related problems, general psychopathology, and salient features of attention deficit hyperactivity disorder.

These researchers believe that Pathway 1 gamblers do not come to gambling with preexisting conditions like depression, bipolar disorder, or impulse dysfunction. When they succumb to addictive gambling, it is a consequence of the inherent addicting nature of gambling's delivery of reinforcement (external cues) and their internal belief system and self-conversation about the potential to win. According to Blaszczynski and Nower, some of these problem gamblers can even eventually gamble "normally."

Pathway 2 gamblers carry with them the consequences of dysfunctional childhoods, along with deficits in effective neurotransmitter function and behavioral controls. Pathway 3 gamblers include people with serious behavioral and impulse control disorders, coaddictions, and disrupted and/or damaged brain neurotransmitter systems. Both Pathway 2 and Pathway 3 gamblers who have crossed the line can never again gamble "just for fun." As a woman with obsessive-compulsive disorder, childhood posttraumatic stress disorder (PTSD), and a near-inability to delay gratification, I walk both pathways. As do many of my friends in Scheherazade's Sisters and the meeting rooms of twelve-step programs.

The pathways model seems valuable for treatment professionals and clients alike. It suggests that for Pathways 2 and 3, more than just stopping and taking part in a support group may be necessary: medication, specifically defined behavior and cognitive modification programs, and the support of a therapist are a few of the recommended tools.

Blaszczynski and Nower are not the only gambling addiction theorists to propose categories of problem gamblers. There is often debate about the differences between the social gambler, the heavy gambler, the problem gambler, and the full-on addict. Some researchers define the inability to stop gambling as a compulsion; others label it addiction. I suspect our prejudices about addiction may motivate the former distinction. And I remember how often I've heard "normies" say, "But it's not a true addiction like alcohol. You're not putting anything into your body." I always answer, "Tell it to my brain chemistry."

My best guess is that those with the genetic predisposition for addiction are on their way to full addiction with the first bet they place. My second guess is that almost every woman gambler who crosses the line into addiction walks, as I do, the second and third pathways. And she knows just when she walked over the line into full addiction.

Let's now consider the gender differences in the pathological gambling patterns of men and women. Men usually begin a pathological gambling pattern during their teens, while women are more likely to become compulsive gamblers when they are older.

Additionally, men are more likely to engage in action gambling (table play, roulette, sports betting), while women typically play slot machines, video poker, or bingo. Action gamblers play for the rush, the high, and the big money. While bingo can provide social interaction for women, slots and video poker serve mostly as a means to escape into one's own world. The onset of gambling addiction with action play can range from ten to fifteen years. Most slot machine and video poker addicts are hooked within a year or two.

Only recently have women compulsive gamblers come to the attention of medical and psychological researchers. Feminist psychologists and theorists transformed the study of human thought, emotions, and behavior in the mid-1970s. For the first time, researchers started to study women—and not just with the traditional laboratory methods, but through women's stories.

Old sexist definitions of emotional and mental dysfunctions were evaluated and revised. My favorite change was when hating housework ceased to be used as a marker for depression in women!

For years, there was little emphasis on the woman gambler, and most researchers were men. That has changed. Contemporary pioneering women theorists, clinicians, and gambling treatment experts opened the way for today's research and therapeutic theory on women compulsive gamblers. Dr. Natasha Dow Schüll and Dr. Nancy Petry (among others) focus their current work on the gender conditioning and pressures that can move a woman toward gambling addiction. Consultant and trainer Joanna Franklin works within the twelve-step framework in teaching clinicians about women gambling addicts. Carol O'Hare, executive director of the Nevada Council on Problem Gambling, has drawn on her own experience as a gambling addict to create outreach and programs for other compulsive gamblers. "Gambling wasn't my problem, life was," she says. She compares the woman video poker addict to a woman slipping into a bubble bath while the cares of the day slip away.

These researchers and treatment/recovery experts suggest that there are characteristics specific to women gamblers that come into play in both the establishment of the addiction and for the best hope of recovery. The next chapter, "Girls Night In," will draw on the work of these women psychologists and others.

A month or so after the Sisters and I explored the function of brain chemistry in our gambling, I take the ideas I have been gathering on psychological underpinnings to our next meeting. I am reluctant to take on the role of an expert, though my enthusiasm for the subject matter helps ease me into it. Still, I feel more like a kindergartener than an expert. I think back on the last four years of my fourteen years of slot play, and I see the relentless cycles of crazy fun and withdrawal. I see a woman who fooled herself into thinking she knew what she was doing—and who blithely ignored her intellectual knowledge.

When I tell the sisters how I feel, Delfina laughs. "Right. You and me. The former counselor and the current social worker. The big experts. Here we are."

Candace nods. "Hey, I basically worked in the belly of the biz. I knew all the tricks, all the ins and outs. Lenny taught me how to count and to cheat. And here I am."

"Okay," I say, "I can live with it. We'll start with the Big Daddy of Psychology—Freud. Take Freud. Seriously, take Freud!"

"No thanks," Sharon says, "my women's studies professor wayyyyy back in 1981 filled us in on Freud. I don't think he liked women much. All that stuff about penis envy. And talk about fairytales, all those wicked mothers destroying their children. Besides, he did cocaine, and we know what that means."

I focus on Freud's constructs of the id, ego, and superego and give short shrift to his theory about gamblers' wanting to lose to punish themselves for desiring their mothers. Nonetheless, Nora crosses her fingers in front of herself and says, "Gag me with a misogynist!"

"That idea's crazy," Barb says, "but he might have gotten it right about all of us having a wild little kid, an adult, and a control freak inside of us. I remember that when I was first gambling

I always felt like a happy kid, especially if it was a long binge with comps for the buffet and those goofy little prizes the slot clubs give out. I still have a skeleton Beanie Baby I got one Halloween. Then the adult in me would sensibly consider that I'd gone to the ATM three times, tell me to eat, go outside, and walk around. Sometimes I listened; sometimes I didn't.

"Later, when I got home and had the nerve to find out what wasn't in my checking account, the control freak kicked in—and she was mean. I'd beat myself up good, which would then make me want to go back and gamble. By the last year, there was no adult. There was only the scared wild child and the punisher."

I move on to talk about Jung's writing Bill W. that an addict's healing had to be guided by something other than intellect and will.

Barb picks back up, saying, "I like what Carl Jung believed about how we humans operate. He understood that we were more than Freud's notions. He believed in the importance of connecting body, mind, and soul."

Helen nods. "Okay," she says, "that makes sense to me. By the end, I knew gambling was hurting my soul. My mama used to talk about a lady who had gotten in married man trouble. She said the devil ate her soul. That last casino disaster I couldn't get my mama's words out of my mind."

"We *are* soul work," Nora says. "Back when I was still gambling, I was desperate for answers to help me stop. There were times when the slot machine was really hitting, and I felt completely whole. Body, mind, and the game in perfect sync. But there was always something missing."

"We have those teachings about wholeness in my religion," K-Siu says. "I was taught not only must we be whole within ourselves, but we are part of a whole that is the world—animals, plants, rocks, air, water, and us all the same."

I tell the group about Jung's ideas of the power of symbols. "I know he was right," I say. "How many of you have favorite machines? I do. It has to do with the images on them. I wouldn't play in a casino that didn't have Cleopatra or Queen of the Nile. The icons are gorgeous: Cleopatra's drag queen eyes, the lotuses, ankhs, the golden Pharaoh and Sphinx, the golden pyramids with light shooting out their tops. I named one of my cars Cleo because the dashboard lights reminded me of that slot."

"Sun and Moon," Sharon says. "I loved Sun and Moon. It has Aztec symbols. I studied Central and South American archaeology and anthropology while I was in college. When the five suns and moons fell into place, I knew I was going to get fifty free spins, with each hit multiplied by two. I once lost 1,000 bucks on one of those machines because it was the only one in the casino and I was afraid that if I went somewhere else to play, somebody else would get on it and not leave."

"The roulette wheel," Candace says. "It was absolutely mysterious and glamorous to me. I probably saw too many James Bond movies."

K-Siu nods. "I told you how beautiful the Bau cua ca cop dice are—a fish, prawn, crab, rooster, calabash gourd, and stag. When they fall in certain winning patterns, it's as though my mind falls into place."

Helen shakes her head. "I would have said this was all New Age mumbo jumbo once upon a time, but I keep remembering that I Dream of Jeannie machine. When the bonus kicked in, I felt like I was opening Ali Baba's treasure chest."

"TOD," Sharon says. "Time on device. That's what the dedicated slot junkie is going for. You reach a point where any win is just more TOD."

"The zone," Delfina says, "I really loved the zone."

I tell the group that there's still more to talk about, but not before we take a much-needed break.

We disband. Candace and Delfina go out front for a cigarette. I go to the back patio and sit under a sky crisscrossed with plane lights. I'm thinking about all the hours I spent in traditional psychotherapy. All the money, all the talk. It wasn't until I began working with a behavioral therapist that I was able to take the first baby steps toward real change. The talk therapy had its value—I know it kept me alive and functioning until I could finally face the reality of the damage in my childhood and the perhaps-greater reality that I am an addict. For that I am grateful. Now the immutable facts of my brain chemistry and how outside stimuli control my behavior—along with Scheherazade's Sisters—are the guiding forces behind not making that first bet, and the discomfort that inevitably follows. As I sit there thinking, I'm already anxious to get back to the circle. Sharing my findings and the feelings it's bringing up is like a lifeline for me in this moment.

When I walk back in, everyone is already seated. "More, please," Candace says. "I'm starting to make sense of some questions I've had for a long time."

"Good," I say, "me, too. I want to talk about behavioral psychology. In some ways it's the most down-to-earth and sensible approach to changing our behaviors, but first, I learned that treatment professionals and researchers often disagree about the definition of a gambling addict. Is a heavy gambler who likes to play for fun an addict? How about a professional gambler who earns her living gambling? What if somebody plays a lot, but doesn't lose much? At the end of the day, it doesn't matter much, though, does it? I know how and when I crossed the line. I bet each of you does, too."

Sharon looks at me and says, "I just read an article in *The New York Times* by a woman whose son is, ahem, a professional online Texas Hold 'Em poker player."

We all groan.

"Right," Sharon says, "she thought that because he sometimes came out ahead that he was a professional earning his living. She needs to read GA's Twenty Questions. Everything she wrote about the kid made it clear that he would have answered yes to eighteen of them—and probably lied about the ones he said no to."

"She also might have believed he was in control of what he was doing," I say, "and could stop any time he wanted."

"Exactly," Sharon concurs. "After all, he kept telling her that."

"Kinda like a rat hitting a lever for food," I say, grateful for the segue. "Welcome to behaviorism."

I fill the Sisters in on the basics. They get it fast. Sharon narrows her eyes. "And you better believe that those computer geeks programming the machines for the casino know every rule in Skinner's book. They create reinforcement schedules to take us down to extinction—*extinction*—that's how the casino industry describes the programming. And we don't know what hit us. We're just girls who gotta have fun."

"I remember my counselor telling me that addiction is the only disease that tells us we don't have a disease," Delfina says. "Behaviorism tells me that we are also perfectly ordinary creatures who can be counted on to respond to rewards and punishments."

"It's almost funny," I say. "Behaviorists use the term *extinction* to mean when a behavior ceases because of punishment. In the case of an addict, the extinction happens only when we finally run out of money. When I was in the casino I was nothing but a lab rat."

I tell the group about rational emotive behavior therapy and the possibility of changing our thoughts and impulses.

"I had a shrink who taught me that," Nora says. "It worked for some of my obsessive thoughts, but when it came to changing my thinking while I was already gambling, it didn't work."

"There's a reason for that," I say. "The same brain changes that jack up the raw appetite part of our brains suppress the part that thinks logically. I remember being zoned out to the point of coma, my blood sugar screaming at me, 'Get something to eat!'; my bladder whimpering, 'Go to the bathroom!'; my sore butt saying, 'Get out of the casino and walk around!'—and not being able to think my way through not hitting the Bet button, much less getting to my feet and walking away."

Everybody nods. I look at the faces of my Sisters in the circle and think about the psychology classes I taught in the '70s. Most of my students were on fire to learn. Most of them intended to become therapists, counselors, and researchers. Many of them did. I see the same intensity of focus and fascination in the eyes of my Sisters tonight. I am again grateful for strong research, perhaps even more for the willingness of these women to squarely face painful truths.

Next I tell them about comorbidity and share my own OCD and PTSD as examples of how I was already dealing with a wounded brain before I even made my first bet. "I figure I medicated my anxiety and brain flash floods with slot play," I say.

"Me, too," Nora agrees. "I learned that in Narcotics Anonymous. We addicts medicate our feelings and mood swings with whatever works—doesn't matter if we have a diagnosed dysfunction or not."

I think about everything I have used to medicate my feelings—food, romance, booze, work, taking care of other people, fantasy, intensity—gambling. As I've moved farther and farther away from my last bet, I've been stunned by the amount of fear that has arisen. Illogical fear. Terror that I have cancer or Alzheimer's. Terror about getting old, about something happening to my adult kids, my cats, my friends. Fear about renewing my driver's license, seeing a dentist, getting my well-woman checkup. Steady-state anxiety that hums just under the surface—along with an unfocused longing for a fix.

"That's us," Delfina says. "When my husband was fooling around with a neighbor while I was fooling around with Double Diamond, I knew exactly what was going on with the two of them. As long as I could find 100 bucks and there was enough gas in the car to drive to the casino, I didn't care. I could just be alone with my favorite lover: Double Diamond."

I laugh. "You all know my track record with men. I'll never forget one night in one of the little Native American casinos. I'd been single and alone for five years. I was happily punching

Max Bet on Silver Moon. A not-too-bad-looking younger guy sat down at the machine next to me and started chatting me up.

"I turned to him—once and once only—and said, 'Listen pal, I'm here to play, not to talk.' He shook his head, got up, and left."

Helen raises her hand. "Sometimes I wonder if I don't just want to get back to when I was a little girl without any real cares. I didn't really like being a grownup. I still don't. It's nothing much but hard work."

"Me, too!" Delfina cries. "I sat in on an in-service training at my work on addicts. A lot of people who treat gambling addicts believe that we, especially, don't want to grow up. Especially we women who got married right out of our parents' homes, had kids early, and have been taking care of other people all the time— or those of us who had a loco family and had to be the grownup right away."

"That's what I wanted to talk about," Helen says. "That ma-larkey about wanting to lose to punish myself makes me sick. No-body likes to lose. I just wanted to keep playing forever. I'd get so I didn't care if I won or lost as long as there was enough to keep playing. Because when I was playing, I was in my own little world. *Nobody* was the boss of me.

"I didn't have to think about my husband's high blood pres-sure or my daughter's second divorce or my grandson who lives in his computer. It was just me and my machine."

As the group talks, I find myself thinking about my time in a coed therapy group for gambling addicts. So often we women would go out after the group and dig deeper into what we were feeling and what we'd done. None of us had been able to relate to the men's stories of 1,000-buck bets and crazy excitement at the track—or the way their gambling fulfilled their needs to be seen as a big shot. All any of us had ever wanted to do was just disappear into the zone.

"I want to add one more thing," I say, "maybe the most important thing. There is now a lot of research being done by women about women gamblers. Most of the research done in the early days was about men. It was based on action gambling, not slots and video poker. It was based on getting a rush, not getting away! What these women researchers and treatment experts are finding is that our stories are most women's stories."

"Hey," Sharon says, "let's use next week's group for Girls' Night In. I've been thinking about us, and about the women I met in the casinos. I know there's some connection between how I am as a woman and why I loved to play so much."

Every single woman nods. "Even though I grew up partly in a culture so different from most of yours," K-Siu says, "I know I loved being able to go away from my busy life when I gambled."

"Me, too," Ginny says. "I told all of you about how I feel like I've got to be better, to prove something, all the time better. That'll make you want to escape into anything that works."

We close the circle. I drive home again with my head spinning. I need time to sort through everything we've talked about tonight. Lonely as my single life can sometimes be and as much as I love the circle, I'm grateful to be heading to the mesa, where I'll be alone with only the company of my thoughts and the silent night sky.

GIRLS' NIGHT IN

GENDER AND WOMEN'S GAMBLING ADDICTION

For women saddled with an excess of caretaking responsibilities at home and at work, machines offer a mechanical relief from the realm of others' demand, as well as from the equally fraught realm of autonomy. Although women may cultivate an intimate relation with the machine, their play aims above all at a total disconnection from the human, including themselves.

—Natasha Dow Schüll, 2002 working paper

I'm late leaving for Girls' Night In. Boo, my young black cat, decides to assert her adolescent independence. I'd leave her out, but the neighborhood coyote has taken to sauntering into my front yard just after sunset. I can only assume that the leftover fried chicken and spaghetti that I put out on a regular basis has something to do with it. The coyote is a young female, irresistible to me in her ability to shape-shift into a ghost drifting across the twilight desert. She would find Boo a delectable hors d'oeuvre.

I see Boo's tail poking out from under the big yucca. I clang a spoon on an open can of cat food. Boo peers out at me. She's not falling for it. I sit on the stoop and wait. I remember all the times I took off for a gambling run and left the cats with a twenty-four-hour supply of food and water, knowing that would force me to come back before I totally crashed and burned.

Finally, I give in to the whims of the feline universe, mutter "Whatever," and put the cat food in the refrigerator. I go to my desk for my purse and keys and see Boo walking calmly through the front door. I give her and the rest of the gang a few treats, make sure the windows are closed, and leave.

I walk into our circle ten minutes late. I'm just in time for check-in. "Sorry I'm late. If I ever do start to gamble again, it'll be because of one of the damn cats. Boo has reached puberty—at least her brain has, even if her body can't."

I look around the circle. There's a new kid in town, not much older than a teenager herself. She's pale and slender. She twists her hands in her lap. There is a delicate Celtic spiral chain tattooed around her right wrist.

The girl laughs. "That's what my mom says kind of about me, except it's more like my body has reached puberty and my brain's on hold." She flinches. "Sorry, is it okay to say stuff like that? Are there rules?"

"No rules," Candace says. "We want to get to know you whatever way you want."

"Should I tell you a little?" the girl asks. She looks at me. "I don't want to butt in."

"I'm done," I say. "I had a good week. I can feel my brain starting to come alive. Sometimes it's fun; more times it's weird being able to feel all the emotions that were numbed by playing slots."

"Oh," the girl says, "I can't feel anything. I'm not sure I want to."

We are quiet for a long pause, and then Ginny turns to the girl and says, "What new members usually do after their first meeting is write a short biography of their gambling and then read it to the group. One of us can help you with that. But first, it would be good to know a little about you." She smiles gently. "Like your name, maybe?"

The girl takes a deep breath. We do a lot of that in this circle. "I'm Tiffany," she says. "I'm nineteen; I'm in college. I'm so freaked out. I've been playing slots since I was sixteen."

I study her pale face. She could be thirteen. I try to imagine her passing for twenty-one. Maybe with makeup and her fine blond hair swept into a French twist, a cigarette in her hand.

"My girlfriends and me," Tiffany says, "used to get dressed up and go over to the Indian casino. The security guard was usually so busy looking down my friend Mason's blouse that he didn't even notice anything else about us. It was a little trickier when one of the lady guards was on, but by then we were regulars."

Nora nods. "I've got a couple friends who eighty-sixed themselves from that casino. They were supposed to get busted if they even walked in. Both of them would cruise right in without getting stopped. I always figured the guards were working for minimum wage—besides, I got to know a couple, and they were just as hooked as we are."

"Yeah," Tiffany says, "we'd see 'em after they went off their shift, zoning out just like we were. At first it wasn't zoning out. It was so much fun. Mason's sister had a great fake ID, so if any of us hit a jackpot, we sat her at the machine, and she'd show her ID and collect. As if we hit many jackpots! And then one of the kids I hung out with showed me how to get into an online casino. My mom and dad had given me a credit card for school expenses— you know?"

She puts her hands over her face. She's in the habit of ending the majority of her sentences on a high note, as if everything she says were a question. I remember this tendency among my former students, how their voices would rise at the end of what they said, how they would look at me as though they were waiting for affirmation or reassurance. We wait. Scheherazade's Sisters do a lot of waiting—not easy for women with "impulse control" problems. Tiffany looks up.

"By the time my folks caught on to what I was doing, I'd maxed out the card—$5,000 maybe? And bought a stolen card off one of my friends. I'm feeling too freaked out to talk anymore. Maybe one of you can help me with my story, and I'll read it next week?" She begins to cry.

Barb writes her phone number on a slip of paper and tucks it into Tiffany's hand. Tiffany nods.

"Thanks, Tiffany," Sharon says. Helen reaches across and pats the girl's hand. "It's hard, honey. It's real hard. I won't kid you. But if I can do this at my age, you can, too." She hands Tiffany her hankie. Helen is probably the only woman I know who carries a handkerchief. Tiffany buries her face in her hands and sobs.

I envy her. I haven't cried in years. Gambling numbed out my sorrow. Then, as my fear and fury escalated, I wouldn't give anyone or anything the satisfaction of my tears.

Tiffany takes a deep breath and then another. "It's so freakin' stupid," she says. "It all started out as fun with my friends, then by the time it was over I almost never left my dorm room. I'm so freakin' alone right now—even my mom and dad, it's weird with them. Why wouldn't it be? How can they trust me? How can I ever trust me again? I don't even drink or smoke pot or be anorexic or fool around with guys or anything? How did this happen?"

"Girlfriend," Nora says, "if you stick around, you'll learn how it happened. And you'll learn how not to let it happen again. That's not going to be easy. But we'll be here."

Tiffany hunches down in her chair. "Okay." Her voice is barely audible. "Okay, what choice do I have?"

I hear Nora, and I hear Tiffany, and I hear echoes across an abyss. I remember when I first sat down in this group. Nothing up to that point had worked—not even my first experience with a support circle.

Somebody had said something about being there for me. All I'd been able to think of were a handful of friendships with women that had flared up and faded away, times when a good woman friend had started an affair with my partner, times when I'd done the same thing to another woman. My feminism had too often run only theory deep. My first loyalty for most of my life had been to male lovers and friends. I'd looked around the circle and wondered if I would ever trust any of the women, much less all of them. That time had come. I trust not just a few of the Sisters— but all of them.

"Tiffany," I say. She looks up. "Who's your best friend?"

"Nobody," she says. "Now? Right now? Nobody. When I got busted, not one of my friends called or came over. I'm sorry, but right now I hate chicks."

"It's okay," Candace says. "You don't have to trust us or even like us. In all honesty, the only women I really like are sitting in this room."

I can't believe what escapes my lips in response. "I never liked women until I sat in some women's groups in the 1970s. Even then, for a long time, I liked women because I knew I needed to. Then, over the last five years, I felt betrayed by some women and went back to being one of the boys. It was easier. I'm a lot like Candace. Right now in my life? I only trust the women in this room. That's how powerful our connections are for me."

Tiffany is quiet. I want to sink into the floor. Ginny looks at all of us. "Girls' Night In. Looks like we already started it."

Tiffany almost smiles. "You guys are truly weird. You're not even girls. You're women."

We all laugh. "Wait till you hear more of our stories," Helen says.

"What's Girls' Night In?" Tiffany asks.

Helen laughs. "It's funny. Back in the old days—thirty, forty years ago—my friends and I always called each other *the girls*. Our husbands were men, and we were girls.

"We've been talking about what made us gamble like addicts. Mary told us about how our brains work and some shrink theories. Then Sharon said we ought to talk about the connection between our being women and being gambling addicts, so we decided to take tonight to talk about it—being women that is."

"Like women's lib chicks?" Tiffany asks.

Helen leans in close to Tiffany. "See these wrinkles? See these little brown spots on my skin? See my bifocals and hearing aids? Hear my Okie accent? Do I seem like a women's libber to you?"

"Oh," Tiffany says in a mouse voice. She starts to shrink in on herself. Helen pats her hand. "I'm just kidding, honey. You better get used to how we joke in here. We're all inmates in the same loony bin."

"I would like to start," K-Siu says. "My people are tough— and traditional. I don't know how I would actually have been raised back in the village, but my mother taught me about being a woman here. We lived near an army base in North Carolina. Sometimes she would see the American women behaving badly—you know, with men, with drinking—and she would use them to teach me and my sisters how a good woman lived.

"My mother was a survivor. Our village is gone. Many Degar villages were bombed to dust or the people taken to camps. My mother believed all her children needed the traditional ways *and* the ways of our new home country. She taught us that a good woman was a 'good housekeeper,' which meant not only taking care of the house but being good-hearted, faithful, industrious, and honest. In the village, women and men did different work. The women planted the gardens, went into the forests and hills to pick wild plants and medicines, and raised the children while the men hunted. Women and men both wove. The men wove carrying baskets; the women wove the shoulder straps. My mother would laugh when she talked about that and say, 'The men can't carry anything without the help of the women.'"

"As if," Sharon says. Helen snorts. "If I had a dollar for every time I called my girlfriend to go to the casino because I got fed up with my hubby messing up something I'd just gotten all nice and clean, I'd at least have a couple hundred bucks."

K-Siu smiles and continues. "It is the same with us—how the women and men are. But, in this country we were not weaving baskets or straps. My mother told us that we would have to be very clever to do well in America. It was not enough to be a good housekeeper. We would have to go to school and get an education. And we would have to become very smart about money. I decided I would be a good woman by obeying the rules of my homeland and what my mother told me about growing up here. It wasn't easy having one foot in a ghost village and one foot in America. In fact, it became so hard I couldn't sleep. And then a lady friend invited me to play Bunco with some other wives. At first, it was just fun. Then I started planning my whole week around when we would play. It was the only time I could relax. Some Bru ladies were playing Bau cua ca cop. I played Bunco one night a week and Bau cua ca cop one afternoon a week. And then one of them said, 'Let's go over to the casino—that way we can win other people's money.'

"They all went straight to the dice tables. I was walking behind them, and I saw a beautiful colored slot machine with fish and prawns and crabs on the screen. I thought of Bau cua ca cop, and I sat down. I was done worrying about being a good woman."

"A good woman," Nora repeats. "Who knows what that really means?"

Candace laughs. "I know. Pick me." Her laugh is joyless. "A good woman gives head, doesn't raise a stink when her boyfriend stays out all night, hands over the credit cards when he asks, cooks, cleans, does the wash, gives head—oh wait, I said that— and works two jobs to keep her True Love going. No wonder I gambled. Besides, if I was playing blackjack and the dealer was a guy, he and the male players always made me feel special."

"I wonder," I say, "did any of the rest of us gamble to feel special, to get chatted up, to feel a little less alone?"

All the other women in the circle shake their heads—even Tiffany. "Anything but," Nora laughs. "You know, there are plenty of available dykes in casinos, but I didn't want anybody bothering me for any reason."

"Guys?" Barb starts in. "You know my story. I'd put on one of my beat-up sweat suits, without a bra, my worst skanky flip-flops, wipe off my makeup, rat's-nest my hair, and I was set. *Nobody* male talked to me.

"I had more than enough men in my life—and they all wanted a tit to suck on. I loved it when I was on a slot machine in a row of all women. I loved it even better when I hit a jackpot and a male payout attendant handed me *my* money with nothing more than a 'good for you.'"

"Hang out with people—no way," Ginny says. "I told you how at first my friends and I would plan to make an evening of it, maybe check out the Chippendale boys, eat as much as we could of a killer seafood buffet, catch a little music; we really loved this singer, Damein Lowe—he could tear the roof off a place. We'd be all dancing and carrying on. He used to dedicate songs to us. "Lonely Teardrops," dang, that'd move my body!

"Then I tried a twenty-line nickel slot machine, and I was gone gone gone. I started going by myself, or with another sister who didn't want to do anything but gamble. I actually turned down invitations from the gang. I didn't want any distractions— nothing! And you want to talk about a good woman? My mama taught me to not expect one damn thing from a man because he'll only let you down. So you gotta be Wonder Woman.

"But now I know my mama was wrong. My husband is a good man. He's all about bringing home the bacon *and* frying it in the pan! He's a better cook than I am and a great dad *and* my best friend. But that old training sticks like glue. *A good sister's gotta be the best—at everything.* See, an African American woman is walking in two worlds, just like K-Siu. I gotta be the best mom to my kids; best wife, lover, and friend to my man; get the most blue ribbons for being Super Teacher at parents' night at my school; always show up to mentor my Little Sister; bake the best sweet potato pie for the choir potluck; lose ten pounds; dress sharp; be there—always—if one of my friends needs something. The casino was the one place I could be plain old Virginia Sampson."

"Be plain old me and not be labeled," Helen concurs. "I get it. I haven't said a word of what I'm going to tell you to anybody. I hate getting old! You all don't know yet, but old women either get ignored or get treated like children. If one more grocery clerk looks at me sympathetically after I've bought a quart of milk and asks, 'Will you need help to the car with that, ma'am?' I will bean her with the milk.

"When I was in a bingo hall or on my slot machine, I wasn't an old, helpless bag. I was a queen. 'Course, I could have toppled over from a stroke and nobody would have much noticed, but I'll take that over being humiliated."

"I'm sixty-nine," I say. "I hate being invisible to men, but I loved being invisible in the casino. I've always felt unattractive next to other women—I've been that way since I was little. I'm a perfectly ordinary-looking woman, but I have times when I feel grotesquely ugly—and clumsy—but never in a casino. I'm like you, Barb. I'd get out of bed in the morning in my sweats and flannel shirt, grab a cup of coffee, and head straight to the casino. I'd walk in through those magic doors and know that nobody gave a crap what I looked like. It was pure freedom."

"Guess what?" Sharon pipes in. "I was prom queen twice, a frickin' cheerleader, I weigh 120 pounds at five-foot-seven, and my blond hair is real—and I *always* feel not quite pretty enough. You would not believe the amount of time I used to put into working to look twenty-five. That's where a lot of my perfectionism comes from.

"I remember a time when I was punching the ATM machine with my perfectly manicured fingernail. Every time I saw No Funds Available I felt like I'd been kicked in the gut—*and* I felt like an outlaw. I was not the successful 120-pound businesswoman/wife/yoga student/cook/perfect daughter. I was a crazy-ass loser whose pits stunk like a dock worker's because she was so buzzed.

"I think the reason you see all those yuppie Harley owners is because they want to believe they're bad to the bone—at least for the weekend. Then on Monday, they trot right back to their cubicles and their six-figure incomes.

"Ha! My six-figure income disappeared in a few years of happy slot time. Now, I'm poking around in resale shops, taking the bus to work, and doing my own nails. At least Ramon still cuts my hair. But guess what? I feel more like a woman than the perfect, glossy robot

I was. Once my butt finally hit that ugly casino carpet, I had to let go of more than my money. I look back now, and I see how lonely I was. Okay. Done now. Next thing you know, I'll be crying."

"I'll go," Helen says. "Let me tell you about old ladies and their husbands. Being with you girls got me to start being more honest with my closest friends. Betty, Janet, Nancy are all my age. Marion is five years older. I invited them all over to tea and cookies. The tea had a little rum in it. None of them complained. Once we were nice and relaxed, I asked them, 'Did your lives change after your husbands retired?' Janet looked at me like she was a shark and I was hamburger. 'Helen,' she said, 'nobody asked me that question before. You just made my day.'

"Well, four hours later we'd all had a few more cups of tea. We'd kicked off our shoes. Marion was laughing so hard we thought she'd have a stroke. We had each confessed that we wanted to kill our hubbies on a regular basis. The only time those men gave us a little rest was if they were out golfing, when some football game was on, or when we could drag them to the casino.

"See, most old guys are still being big shots. They don't play slots. So hubby goes off to the card tables, and the little woman gets to do whatever she wants—which, in my case, was to cement myself to the seat at I Dream of Jeannie and bribe Jim with a few bucks every time he came over and wanted to leave. I'm not saying I don't love Jim. But like him? About once a year, if that."

"I like my husband most of the time," Delfina says. "You have to remember that Elizar was my biggest ally about going to college. But I have seen so many Latina women in my clinic who aren't with guys like him. There is this code of machismo in Latin culture that runs really deep. Mr. Husband is the rooster, and *la senora* is the hen. Even Elizar fell for that bullshit for a while: the mistress, the refusing to tell me where he was going or why he'd be away all night. When he was with his *puta*, I knew it. I always knew. And, you better believe me, the only medicine that worked was neon and bells. I could lose myself in my slot machine for as long as it took for me to calm down, go home, and not kill his *pinche cabron culo*."

"What does *culo* mean?" K-Siu asks.

"Butthole."

"So when your husband was unfaithful, he was a fucking butthead butthole?" K-Siu's face is serious for a second, then she doubles over with the giggles.

"That would be it," Delfina says. "You know that walking in two worlds thing and getting it perfect routine is verrrry big for me and *mis chicas*. But let me tell you, when we get ourselves all glamoured up and go out together, we can forget all of it. I'm lucky to have found some new friends who can party without going to the casino. I'd go crazy if it weren't for those ladies."

"Maybe it isn't about backgrounds or nationalities," Nora says, "maybe it's about being second-class to well-off white men. Believe me, we lesbians, especially those of us who are politically active, are definitely walking in two worlds. And talk about perfectionism? My partner and I are total clean freaks. She finally had to make me promise that we'd take one night a week off for a date night. And her job? I had to make her promise that she'd only bring work home six nights a week instead of seven. I'm pretty safe in my line of work, but she's a real estate agent, and between all the whacked-out homophobes in this state and the comatose real estate market, she's gotta be better than the best.

"In my own case, stress was a big part of my addiction. Stress and the cool feeling that I was just another woman when I was in the casino, instead of wondering if people could tell that I was a lesbian and hating me for it."

"We were all hiding," I say. "From prejudice, from husbands, from having to be perfect, from exhaustion—maybe from feelings more than anything else."

"And maybe to jack some of the good feelings up," Candace says. "I love to be high. That's part of why I became a dancer. When it's just me and the music, I feel like a goddess. Same deal when I'd hit blackjack or all the right symbols would line up on my slot machine. The buzzer would go off, and all I had to do was sit there and wait for my money."

"Or," I say, "when the bonus symbols lined up, and I knew I could just sit back and watch the free rounds spin by. All wins multiplied by three. Or four. Or five, depending on the machine. That moment those symbols appeared was like wanting to kiss a guy and realizing he was about to kiss me. Bliss guaranteed.

"But there's something else I keep thinking of when I think about the women I've met in the casinos. There was one time I was playing next to two women who were friends. The one nearest me kept trying to take care of the other one. She'd get her drinks, bring back a bag of chips, cash in her nickel buckets for her—this was back in the old days before they started using paper payout slips. The other woman was terribly thin. Her hair looked like it was plastic. She was chain-smoking. The emaciated woman got up to go to the ladies' room, and her friend turned to me and said, 'Thanks for not staring at her. I tried to tell her to get a decent wig, but she didn't want to waste the money. She's dying of cancer. She's got maybe six months to live.' I was, for once in my life, without words.

"'Some people might judge her,' the woman said, 'but let me tell you, playing slots is the only thing that takes the pain away— the physical and the mental.'

"I remember looking at the woman and saying, 'She's lucky to have you.' We turned back to our machines, and when I next looked over, they were both gone."

Ginny nods. "I used to get these crazy tension headaches. All it took was ten minutes on my favorite machine, and the worst splitting pain was gone."

"There was another woman," I say. "I've never told anybody about her, not in any of the other groups, not the therapy group even. It seemed like it would be violating her privacy. But tonight I'm wishing she could be with us. I doubt she's even still alive. I was playing at the little Indian casino around eleven at night. There was somebody on my favorite machine, so I went to a bank of slots I'd never played. There was an empty Halloween machine. It's my favorite holiday, so I figured it was a sign. I sat down, shoved in a ten, and started getting lost. I told you I didn't normally talk to people, but the woman next to me said, 'Don't you just love gambling?' in this eerie, whispery voice. I looked at her. She had silvery-blond hair and an almost-Barbie-doll body. She'd outlined her eyes in black, old hippie chick style. Her voice was young, but her face was as withered as a ninety-year-old's.

"'I look like shit, don't I?' she said and grinned.

"'What?' I said. She laughed. 'It's okay. I know I do, but it's not too bad for somebody who's got maybe a year to live—tops.'

"'Cancer?' I asked. You know how you can sometimes just open right up to another gambler.

"'Cancer,' she concurred. 'My own fault. Ovarian. They didn't catch it early because I'm scared of doctors, so I never got my exams like you're supposed to. They got it out of my ovaries, but it went everywhere.' My husband bailed. My sister takes the kids most nights. She thinks I'm going to support groups, but piss on that. I come *here*. Because playing these machines is the only thing that takes the pain away. More better, while I'm playing I can forget I'm dying.'

"Just then, I swear it, she hit a 50-buck jackpot and I hit 35. We high-fived. She lit up a cigarette and grinned. 'Hey, I can smoke all I want. They ain't gonna kill me.'

"My machine was hot for maybe half an hour. Then, of course, it went cold. I stood up. 'Time to leave,' I said. 'It was good to talk,' the woman said. Then she reached up and hugged me. I can still smell her scent—a subtle perfume. I hugged her back. It was the first time I'd shared touch with anyone in three years."

"God," Tiffany says. "That's a true story, isn't it?"

"It is," I say. "I'm glad for her. I'm glad she found something to help her make it through. A friend told me that his dad works in hospice in Phoenix. His dad said that he's surprised by how often his hospice patients say they would go to the casino if they could do anything they wanted. It doesn't surprise me."

We decide to take our break. Tiffany stops me at the door. "Can we go talk a little bit outside? I gotta have a cigarette, but there's something I need to tell somebody."

"Happy to," I say.

We go out onto the little scruffy patio. There are three struggling palm trees. The sun is dropping fast in the west. The days are growing shorter. It's been a year since I was in Tiffany's shoes.

Tiffany sits on the ground in the shade of the thickest palm, leans back, and lights up. I pull a chair over. "You were a shrink, right?" she asks. "Not really," I say, "I was a counselor."

"But you listened to people, right? That's what Nora told me."

"I listened to people," I say.

"Could you listen to me for a minute?"

"Absolutely," I say.

"Okay. So, what if a person did some bad things because they had to get money because otherwise some other people who they owed money to were reallllly going to mess them up?"

I'm quiet for a minute. Tiffany crushes her cigarette out in the sand. "You hate me, right?"

"No way," I say, "I was just trying to gather my thoughts. First off, I'd figure that person wanted to live. Second off, I'd be happy to listen more. Third off, I'd probably tell that person who wanted to live that she might want to get a checkup at the woman's clinic just to make sure everything's okay."

"I made them use a condom," she says. "There were maybe only five times—and I took the money and gave it to the people who would have messed me up, and they left me alone, you know?"

She looks up at me. "So, my so-called friends? The chicks that turned me on to the casino in the first place? They called me a skanky ho, and they said they'd never speak to me again."

"You know what?" I say. "You got lucky on that!"

Tiffany laughs. "I did." The question mark is gone. She pulls a brush out of her backpack and smoothes her hair. "I feel a little better," she says. "But I got a long way to go."

"Don't we all," I say. "Don't we all."

Sharon opens up the second half of our circle. "There's a stereotype about the woman gambler just like there are stereotypes about women drunks. I remember when I was a kid and my folks would go to Vegas for a weekend. My mom would come back and say—every time—'Those poor old women. They're just glued to their slot machines. They look so lonely and miserable.'"

Helen snorts. "Not quite."

"My dad used to shake his head sadly," Sharon says. "He called them *slot hogs*. 'They're so pitiful,' he'd say. 'They all look alike. Their faces are gray; they wear a grimy white glove on their right hand; they look like zombies.'"

"And they didn't even have the perfect accessory—a fanny pack!" Barb says. "Talk about misery."

"All I have to do," I say, "if I may digress, is hear that phrase—*fanny pack*—and I want to head right out the door to the casino. My fanny pack was purple. I embroidered *Holy Fanny Pack* on it in silver thread. I had a climbing carabiner with my slot club cards and my lucky charms clipped to the strap: a silver rabbit, a plastic Hello Kitty, a pair of red dice, and a glow-in-the-dark jackpot chip I'd gotten at the Indian casino. I only used it for gambling. It hung empty on the coatrack until those glorious moments when I'd think, *Fuck it, I'm going.* I'd dump in my spare quarters, the casino coupons I'd gotten in the mail for treats and comps, a Trader Joe's lip balm. . . ."

Nora bursts into laughter. "Omygod," she says, "Me, too. I'd forget to drink water while I was playing, and my lips would dry out. Here's the best part: I've always been a health food nut. I take homeopathic tinctures. I've got a vitamin regimen that takes me five minutes in the morning. I'd never use commercial lip balm—all those unnatural chemicals. So, there I'd sit for three hours, with my back aching, sucking in secondhand smoke, not eating till my blood sugar was in my toes, then grabbing a double cheeseburger at the snack counter while somebody held my machine for me—finish the burger, wipe my lips, and apply my Trader Joe's organic lip balm!"

"Right on, sister," I say. "My purple fanny pack was all part of my ritual. There was the absolute joy of going to the credit union, taking out $200, and asking the teller to give it to me in fives. I'd put the wad into the Holy Fanny Pack, grab a cup of killer cappuccino at my favorite local espresso place, and head out on I-40, the highway to heaven. And when I walked into the casino, took my coupons to the slot club, picked up my bonus bucks and my souvenir, then sat at my machine and opened my well-organized fanny pack? It was nirvana."

Helen high-fives me.

"So," Sharon says, "I'm listening to all of us, and I'm thinking it doesn't matter if a woman is twenty or eighty. Some things haven't changed that much for women. So many women and girls killing themselves to look like Barbie dolls, eleven-year-olds starving themselves to be liked, Wonder Women trying to do everything perfectly, glass ceiling still superglued in place. Mary, I bet you look back on the '70s and '80s and wonder what the hell happened."

"I couldn't have put it better," I say. My tone is dry, but there's sadness in me.

"On top of what we learned and what hasn't changed about being women," Sharon says, "we've also got these outdated stereotypes of who a woman gambler is—the old broad gambling away her loneliness. *And* we get lumped in with male gamblers, instead of it being understood that we're different."

"Well," I say, "there are those few psychologists who are working to change those outdated notions, especially Nancy Petry, Joanna Franklin, and Natasha Dow Schüll. And the big treatment organizations—GA, the Council on Problem Gambling, gambling addiction divisions of state and federal health departments—are bringing attention to the rapidly increasing numbers of women in the problem gambling population. I think part of the reason we don't see a lot of information about women gamblers in the media is because scientific research is slow to make it into the popular press, while the number of casinos is multiplying exponentially fast, *and* the industry's ability to technologically manipulate slot machines is skyrocketing."

"Rats in a maze," Ginny says. "Sister rats in a maze."

We switch to talking about our lives over the last week. Our stories are similar: Sometimes we sit through intense gambling urges, get triggered by TV or twilight, discover a new or forgotten fascination in an ordinary moment in life. Some of us are paying off credit cards or finally being able to take out a loan. We start to close the circle. Ginny seems lost in thought. She looks up and says, "I've got one more thing to say about the woman stuff. I suddenly remembered something that had a huge influence on my gambling. I've been thinking about my father. We had parent conferences last week at my school. Sometimes parents bring their kids. I saw how thrilled the girls were when their fathers came. It's usually only the moms who show up. It made me think about how much I loved it when my dad paid attention to me.

"He was, not often, but often enough, a lot like my husband—hardworking, kind, and loving. But he was a gambler, and by the time I was in my teens he was a slave to it. I forgot until just now how he took me with him to the casino a few times when I was maybe nine or ten. That was back in the days before they got real strict about kids being on the gambling floor. Even after all I've gone through, I remember those times like it would the best kind of Fourth of July. Family and fireworks and all the good, greasy food you could eat.

"He never took my brothers or other sisters. It was just me and him. I wonder if it was because there were times when my mom would get religion and refuse to go.

"Me and my daddy, we were golden. He was well-known, so the dealers and waitresses and floormen all treated me like a little princess. The cocktail waitress would bring me Shirley Temples with little paper umbrellas in them. The restaurant staff all knew my dad and me, and they'd give me crayons and a stack of paper placemats. The cook would fix me macaroni and cheese soul-style.

"Sometimes, we'd stay overnight. My dad had three lifetimes' worth of comps. I'd get my own room. The hotel staff knew I was in there and kept an eye on me. I wasn't one bit scared. Sometimes I'd stay up most of the night, looking out the big windows on the lights of Las Vegas and feeling like an angel high in the sky.

"My dad would always come in to kiss me goodnight, even if it was four in the morning. And, no matter how late he'd stay up, we'd be out the door for the breakfast buffet at 8:00 AM. There wasn't anything weird about it—you know—like a daddy who likes his little girl too much. But it left me loving that casino magic. I've looked for it since then, and I bet I'll look for it the rest of my life."

Tiffany calls me on my cell while I'm driving home. "I'm scared," she says. "I'm at my folks' place, in my bedroom. I tried to explain a little to them. They just told me to pray. I feel so alone. Being with you ladies was the first time I haven't felt like a total freak in so long."

"Do you want me to come over?" I ask.

"No," she says. "I just needed to hear a few voices from the circle. I'm going to call Candace, too. I'll come back next week, I promise."

I laugh. "I know you will. You might not know it yet, but you've got just what it takes to beat this thing. You're open. You cry. And you're not afraid to call for support. You can email me, too. Write me, and I'll send you some stuff that's helped me get through. Sometimes, you might not be able to reach any of us by phone, and it helps to just log on and get reminded of what works—and what doesn't."

We say goodnight. I drive through the sweet desert dark thinking of my freshman year in college—September in 1958. I was eighteen. I'd been there four days when I woke just before midnight in my dorm room unable to breathe, in terror because I didn't know who I was. My dorm adviser was kind, but in those days no one knew much about anxiety disorder, PTSD, separation anxiety, or depression—much less how a young woman who'd been her mother's mom might feel the loss of that role as utter annihilation.

I'd crouched on a sofa in the common room while my adviser calmed me down. A few other girls had walked by and given me curious looks. By the next day, I was an outcast. By the weekend, I had been transferred to a dorm for "troubled" girls. There was no counseling. I managed to garner enough from the other girls' stories to know I wasn't going crazy. And then I put any healing I might have done on hold. I seduced a decent young man and within four months was married and thrown out of college.

I pull into my driveway. Boo, the errant black kitten, sits in the window watching. I turn off the car and, as has become my practice after the circle, sit in the yard in the perfect quiet. I wonder how different my life might have been had I found a group like Scheherazade's Sisters when I was eighteen—not to heal from addiction, but to learn I was not alone.

GET HER TO SIT DOWN

THE INDUSTRY'S STRATEGIES
TO KEEP WOMEN PLAYING

G Casino Women's Networking Lunch, Thursday 8th October 09. For women who want to network and meet other like-minded women. G Casino, Westwood Cross are holding a women's networking lunch. . . .

—U.K. casino advertisement

My friend Lee Barnes is a dangerous writer, a man of elegant and precise words. He's also a former card dealer and croupier. He worked casino tables in the '70s in downtown Vegas. I sought Lee out when I started researching industry strategies. I wanted to learn about how the casino corporations control gamblers; how computer experts design Machiavellian programs within slot machines; how casino architects, designers, and public relations people create the gambling industry's glittering leg-hold traps. And I specifically wanted to understand how this played out for women.

My friend laughed when I threw in this last qualifier. "It's pretty simple," he said. "Get her to sit down. Especially slot players."

"They didn't have to persuade me," I said. "My happy place was a glowing screen with a voracious appetite for money."

"They had you," Lee said. "They get your reticular activating system hooked into visual repetition, and their profits are guaranteed."

I think of Lee's words as I dive into my writing, into the often-no-less-insidious screen of my computer: *Get her to sit down.* That's also one of the first rules for any woman who wants to write. I log on, and it's Research Time.

One of the gifts of my obsessive brain is an immoderate love for research. I type "casino design" into Google search and am taken into a world as dazzling as any casino. The websites of the businesses serving the gambling industry hold powerful clues to what drives casino marketing, design, and technology. They—the interior designers, architects, carpet manufacturers, slot machine fabricators, uniform designers, public relations firms, and others—all provide a double service: guarantee maximum profit *and* pitch their machinations to the gambler as "services," promising to make "gaming" an enjoyable, comfortable, and alluring experience.

Even the advertising of the most peripheral businesses is a hook for me. The glitzy images of casino interiors, promotional postcards, slot club cards, and advertisements make me want to log off, shut down the computer, grab my wallet, and drive toward perdition. That urge is a tribute to casino marketers—and the persistence of my torqued neurochemistry. It's a greater tribute to Scheherazade's Sisters that I sit tight and keep working.

A couple of ten-hour days later, I log off and go to the mirror. I look at my bleary-eyed reflection and say, "You were a rat in a maze. A happy rat most of the time, but a rat nonetheless." I watch myself grin. I have often wished that looking back on my gambling years would provoke feelings of embarrassment, regret, even anger. Instead, I am always longing—for the way my heart leaped the instant I thought *I'm going*, for the heedless joy I felt every second on the way to the casino, for the sheer relief that flooded me as I slid my first five into the bill receiver and hit Bet.

I have known ever since I began listening to the other women in Scheherazade's Sisters that I got off easy. I never contemplated suicide. I never lost my family. I never went to jail. I didn't lose my home, my mink coat, my beloved diamonds, my stellar credit rating—mainly because I didn't own anything. I didn't end up in a psych unit pumped full of mood stabilizers or antidepressants. Up until the migraine auras began, my time in casinos was nothing but fun—at least till I woke the next morning.

I look my mirror self in the eye. "How about those predawns you jolted awake in a casino hotel room?" I say. "Remember? Your heart pounding in your brain. Your brain shrieking *Get me out of my body.*" My reflection shrugs.

"Hey," she says, "you play, you pay—besides, you were the victim of operant conditioning. You were a rat. You loved it." She laughs. "And you know what? The whales? The mega mega rich gamblers the big casinos suck up to? They're rats, too."

I've always liked the gambler in me. She was a hell of a lot more fun than the person who showed up when I was in my immediate withdrawals—even more fun than the person I am in my ongoing abstinence. If we'd sat next to each other playing slots, I might have deigned to talk with her. She was a funny wiseass. She was both deluded and clearheaded. And her politics were impeccable.

Even to this day she isn't angry about what we lost in the casinos—time, money, more than a few brain cells—but she becomes an avenging goddess when she remembers how the employees of casinos were treated—especially the guys and gals in the trenches.

"Okay," I tell her, "I'm going to write about the unswerving intention of the casino industry—their steadfast commitment to making as much money as they can with equally steadfast disregard for the human consequences of their obsession."

She gives me a high-five. I go into the kitchen to start dinner. I'm going to need fuel for the long writing hours ahead.

Here is a sensory tour of eighteen hours in the life of a gambling addict—specifically a woman far from being a whale, specifically me. We don't begin with walking into the casino. We begin on a muggy July morning in any year from 1999 to 2008, in a little cabin at the edge of a fragrant ponderosa pine forest in Northern Arizona. There are crows and Steller's jays playing circus in the dark trees and wildflowers spangling the summer grasses like fallen stars. That's where I found myself, but we could be talking about any location on Planet Casino: Nevada, Atlantic City, in a revitalized Colorado mining town, on a Southwestern desert reservation or a faux Mississippi riverboat. For the compulsive gambler, everywhere is only a pit stop on the way to the casinos. To occupy Planet Casino is to leave one's real home behind.

I have drunk coffee, sat on the back deck, and said my meditation. I've heated up waffles, eaten, washed my plate, and checked email. I open the article I'm writing, stare at it for fifteen minutes, and log off. There are no messages in my voice mail. It's too early to go for a walk. I'm bored with most of my friends. I'm bored with my life.

I play computer Scrabble for an hour till the mailwoman pulls up to the boxes in her old pickup. I suffer always from "anticiparcelation," a term my youngest son and I created to describe those who always believe there will be a wonderful surprise in the mail.

I check the mail. There are a couple of bills, the *Flagstaff Women's Newsletter*, a monthly magazine my friend the Aradia Bookstore owner puts out—and there is a big, gaudy postcard that looks like it was designed by an ancient Puebloan infatuated with Day-Glo ink. My throat goes dry. Life is suddenly fascinating.

I take the mail to my back deck and read the postcard. *!!Midsummer Madness!! We've gone crazy at Mystic Mesa! $10,000. Mystery Bonus for one lucky Money Maniacs slot club player!* There's a picture of a sturdy older gal in harlequin motley. She waves handfuls of hundred-dollar bills in the air.

All I have to do is play at my favorite machine with my lucky Money Maniacs slot club card, and I could be the lucky One. Plus, if I take the postcard to the Money Maniacs slot club, I'll be given a voucher good for $15 in free play *and* a chance to win up to $1,000 with a free spin on the Money Maniacs Only roulette wheel.

I dump the bills and newsletter on my desk and shut down the computer. I square the cats away with food and water, call my neighbor, and tell him I might be away on business overnight. "Hey," he says, "every now and then you gotta shake the dust off your shoulders." He knows me.

I grab my Holy Fanny Pack, stuff in my lucky nickel bag, lucky Trader Joe's lip balm, lucky dark glasses, and my slot card on its long, coiled bungee cord. I flash for a second on something a good friend once told me about his cocaine years: "I think I liked all the cool paraphernalia as much as I liked the drug." I think of Robert Downey Jr. saying, "It's like I have a loaded gun in my mouth and my finger's on the trigger, and I like the taste of the gunmetal." *That's me*, I think, and scoot out the door.

I check the gas. I've got barely enough to make it to the casino. I consider just hitting the road. Despite my wicked outlaw ways, I decide I better give myself a little safety net. I make myself stop at the local gas station. Even putting gas in the tank is exciting. Taking 200 bucks out of the ATM is a rush. I grab a puny convenience store coffee and a stale jelly donut. Then I am on the road, driving south, and the coffee and roll taste like the finest cappuccino and pastry.

Forty-five minutes later (thirty if it's a good day and there are no cops), I turn off the highway onto the frontage road and drive to the Mystic Mesa Casino and Luxury Hotel. It's easy to find my way in. There are abundant, vivid, and alluring signs; my favorites are a series posted at the turn into the huge parking lot. They are written not by a marketing department, but by the actual casino workers—the waitresses, change people, keno runners. Today's says:

Come out of the sun
You might be the One
To "cash" in on the Fun!

Yeats, Basho, Mary Oliver?—those poets are great, but this poem is genius.

If I were rich, I'd drive up to valet parking, leave my vintage classic Firebird, and saunter toward the entrance doors. Since I'm me, I drive out to the edges of the vast parking lot, where I can camp in my beat-up Vibe overnight should my adventure prove unprofitable. Though some casinos provide a shady multistory parking garage, I've learned the hard way how a motorcycle roar at three in the morning can jolt me into insomnia.

I park, gather up the Holy Fanny Pack, and climb out into sledgehammer heat and glare. I can feel the asphalt burn through the soles of my sandals. The casino entrance gleams cool as an oasis. I check the location of the Vibe for my return trip. I've learned this from experience, because at the end of the evening the walk out of the casino is boggling to a gambling-altered mind.

Since there are no signs marking the parking lot rows, I fix details in my mind: far southwest corner of lot, near a withered juniper, within a hundred feet of the entrance to the outdoor music amphitheater. Those will be my last responsible and even mildly coherent thoughts for the next ten hours.

I race to the edge of the parking lot, step onto the sidewalk, and stroll the last few hundred feet to the doors. I pretend to take my time, as though I'm admiring the wilting flowers, the fake waterfall pouring over fake boulders, the scarlet PT Cruiser glittering like a bloated ruby on its display stand, the sign above it that reads: *Take me home. Midsummer Madness Cruising to Glory Slot Tournament.*

Slowing down heightens my anticipation. My mouth is dry; my heart speeds up. After days and weeks of feeling not-quite-right, I feel completely myself. Life is good! I pause to examine a wilting geranium and have a moment of honesty with myself. I also slow down because I don't want to look like a desperate slot junkie.

The huge doors are smoked glass etched with two petroglyph-style Ms. I pause, look in, and see a mirage of jeweled neon. Even though I'm hot and sweaty, I wait to open the door. I love this moment. Even more, I love the next. I push both doors open.

A wave of chill, smoky, ionized air washes over me. The security guard stands behind her podium reading something. She looks up and waves. "Welcome back, girl!" I grin and step onto the carpet. While I have walked into a visual cacophony of neon and glitter, The Carpet has a stunning glory of its own. It's gold, turquoise, and royal purple—the security guard once told me, "It's a desert twilight theme"—and it's printed with dice, slot machines, cards, and roulette wheels. "It jazzes you up," the guard said, "and it doesn't show the dirt!"

The sweet din of buzzers and bells, of shouts and laughter and tinny oldies rock 'n' roll surrounds me. I breathe in casino air. I can't stop grinning. I am home.

I make myself think the next two minutes through: Go to the Money Maniacs Slot Club counter and check my comp points; hand in the postcard the casino sent and collect a coupon for 15 bucks; play the complimentary roulette wheel; go to the restaurant and grab soup and coffee to go; then walk slowly through the casino, scoping out which machines are free, and make my choice.

Five seconds later, I see that there is no one playing my favorite slot, a machine that is coveted by many players. I hotfoot it to the slot, tip the player chair against it, put an ashtray on the chair to reserve the machine, pray no novice sees the machine and doesn't know the slot hog signal that a machine is taken. I race to the cashier, convert my two hundred into fives, and hustle back to my machine. Nobody has claimed it. I dump my slot club coupons back in the Holy Fanny Pack, settle down, and shove a five into the bill receiver. I figure I'll grab a coffee and a grapefruit juice from the cocktail person. There's a bag of cashews in the Holy Fanny Pack. Nuts are protein, right?

At first, I play my system: 5 bucks at a time, cash out the instant I'm up even $1, stay no longer than thirty minutes on one machine, check out all my favorites, and repeat the routine; when my cash is gone, take all my payout slips to the cashier and get brand-new money.

Things go smoothly for the first couple of hours. My system is working. I've hydrated and caffeinated with free beverages. I've eaten the cashews and made myself go to the ladies' room before my bladder threatens to explode. I'm up 60 bucks from my $200 nut.

I go to glance at my watch. My wrist is bare. I'd deliberately not put the watch on. Checking the time is not for a hedonist. There's no point in looking for a clock in the casino or a window to gauge the hour. There are no clocks, no windows, and the smoked glass in the front and back doors creates perpetual twilight outside.

I could eat a healthy meal, but the restaurant is alllll the way across the casino floor. I could take a break outside, but it might still be scorching, and the cool air feels great. I could catch some tunes in the show lounge, but I hear a voice on the sound system. "Congratulations to Jackie. She just won $5,000." I can listen to music anywhere.

I go to the snack bar and ask the counter guy to make me my special high protein, high potassium milkshake. He grins. "Don't tell me, I remember you from last week. Skim milk, one scoop of vanilla, one banana, and blend it till the chunks are gone."

"You're good," I say.

"Hey," he says, "I'm not gonna forget a generous lady like you." He laughs. "Besides, you're a regular. You know the deal; they train us to remember faces."

I make myself sit on the counter stool and wait. There's a burst of noise from a nearby table. The waiters and waitresses are Lindying to "Rock Around the Clock." They finish, bow, and sing happy birthday to a beaming little kid sitting with his family. The parents look like they've been up for a week. A waitress sets a cupcake with a burning candle in front of the kid. He and his parents lean in to blow the candle out.

I spot an empty Adonis machine about ten feet from the snack shop. I start to tell the counter guy I'll be right back, but he's headed my way with a takeout cup and a glass. He pours the remainder of the milkshake in the glass. "Here," he says, "slam this down. I don't want you passing out from low blood sugar before you get back to your machine."

I give him a ten, tell him to keep the change, and head to the ATM and the cashier for another wad of fives. My second-favorite machine is open. I settle in with my resupplied Holy Fanny Pack and the milkshake. Somehow it seems that there has been a change in my good fortune. The machine vacuums up $100 in twenty minutes. It keeps paying me losing wins—five nickels back on a nine-nickel bet and even money on a few bigger bets.

I finish the milkshake and dig in. The woman next to me hits. Sixty bucks. Not a gold mine, but enough to keep me glued to my seat. "Anybody hit big on this one?" I ask. "Nope," she says, "it's going to pop any second. That's what mine did. You know, you get all those chump change hits, then wham!"

I slide in another five. I consider cashing out after this one, but I remember the advice of the drink attendant in a tiny casino up near Kanab, Utah. I'd sunk 80 bucks into my slot, gone to the ladies' room, and come back to find a guy on *my* machine. He was grinning. He had cause to. The machine had just paid him 125 bucks. The sweet-faced drink attendant looked at me sadly and said, "You gotta remember, never leave your machine."

Here, in a comfortable back section of Mystic Mesa Casino, I don't leave my machine for eight hours—except to go to the ATM and pee. I don't eat again. I manage to drag myself to the ladies' room and the water fountain—barely. I gulp down free weak coffee till my hands shake so much I can barely press the ATM or the Max Bet button.

By now, I am a skin bag of raw impulse. Now and then my brain whimpers, "Get up. Take a break." But always, just then, the machine graciously hands over a hot one-hundred- or two-hundred-nickel payout. Or the slot club attendant shows up with a coupon for the snack bar or a voucher for 10 bucks.

Around two in the morning I stop. No miracle has intervened. No amount of reading the sign at the cashier's cage that says WHEN THE FUN STOPS slows me down. None of the effects of my plummeting blood sugar make me stagger to the all-night coffee shop. I stop because the ATM tells me I have no more available funds—not just that I've reached my limit of daily withdrawals, but that there is no more money anywhere in my savings or checking accounts.

I started my Mystic Mesa hike with $853 in my checking account and $206 in my savings. I toss the *withdrawal refused* slips in the trash and head for the Vibe. Just after I'd parked, I'd stashed 40 bucks for coffee and breakfast—and for the sense of virtue I would get from driving home other than dead broke. The gas tank is full. I'll figure out what comes next in the morning. I always think better on decent coffee.

I walk out of the casino. The desert air is a blessing. There's a half moon and coyotes yipping in the distance. I remember my cues to find my car: far southwest corner of lot, near a weather-beaten juniper, within a hundred feet of the entrance to the outdoor music amphitheater.

There are no other cars parked near the Vibe. I pull down the back seats, toss my camping pad onto the platform, and then, just to be sure, I check the glove compartment. The forty is safely tucked away—for about five seconds. The instant I touch the bills, I feel a jolt of optimism.

Quit now? When it's only two o'clock? Quit when there's enough gas to drive home and $20 could turn the tide? It has before. I lock the Vibe and march purposefully back to the casino. My ice-bound slot machine is still free. I convert my forty into fives. I see clearly that the problem has been that I abandoned my fail-proof system. I tip the cashier 5 bucks. The universe loves the generous.

I walk calmly back to the machine and slip in my slot club card and a five. The waitress brings me a fortifying grapefruit juice. Two hours later, I am up 20 bucks. I cash out triumphantly. I am a woman with an IQ of 130-plus and a master's degree in psychology—and I am happy with $20 for two hours' "work." In the old days they called players who gambled till their last dollar was gone *degenerate gamblers*. The casino industry calls it taking the player down to extinction. I am not degenerate, I have not been extinguished, and there is maybe an hour and a half of darkness left, and I now intend to sleep.

Dawn jolts me awake two hours after I fall asleep. I feel as though there are uninsulated high-voltage wires snaking under my skin. My stomach is a knot of the same wire; my thoughts are on bipolar manic. I know what to do. Adjust my brain chemistry. Coffee. Deep-fried carbohydrate. Gamble. Win. Make back what I've lost.

The coffee and donuts work. The fiscal plan doesn't. Three hours later, I drive toward Flagstaff. I'm grateful that I don't feel worse than I do. I'm still a little high. I know it will last for maybe a day. I'll ride it while I can. And then, maybe something will happen. I've still got credit on my five credit cards. I'll pick up a couple new students. I know I am still in a lingering buzz. The crash will come.

I'm sitting at my old rolltop desk on a gorgeous Mojave day. I read what I've written and feel nothing but nostalgia. That's the nature of this dysfunction. The memories of hot wires under my skin and in my gut, the racing thoughts and the crash that always followed, pale against the recollection of the fun—and the way the obsession reduced life to simplicity.

I loved how uncomplicated my choices were in a casino. Eat. Don't eat. Drink coffee. Don't drink coffee. Go the ladies' room. Stay in my seat. Get off Cleopatra. Go to Sun and Moon. Switch to Aztec Gold. Try fives. Try tens. Try twenties. Up my bet. Drop my bet.

I spent twenty years of my life as a working mother and the full support of three kids. My decisions had more often than not seemed a hopelessly tangled skein of threads. Single motherhood, especially on a low income, is like a game of chess for which the stakes are survival or disaster.

I rarely occupied the moment in which I was living. My mind was always five steps behind the game plan. *If the check comes, I'll buy groceries first, then pay the rent, then electricity . . . if the check doesn't come, I'll have to figure out where to get money for tonight's and tomorrow's food . . . if my daughter's sore throat gets worse, I'll have to take her to the clinic and cancel my afternoon appointments . . . if she's better, I need to get her to soccer practice between my last appointment and buying food for dinner, if the check comes. . . .*

What's more, I was a woman gratefully immersed in early second-wave feminism, learning assertiveness, challenging old gender conditioning, pushing through terror to make changes in my perceptions and behaviors. I was a therapist and mental health trainer. Change was my mantra. I was coming to crossroads all the time, questioning my every reaction and impulse, thinking about which way to go. My generation of powerful women invented multitasking—in both our external and our internal lives.

I can't remember more than a few moments of feeling relaxed in two decades of being a working mom. My brain was on overdrive from the second I woke till the second my body fell asleep. So I have an immediate response when people have asked me why, if I loved gambling so much, I didn't just learn to count cards and play blackjack. I have (ask any of my lovers) a piranha memory. My brain gobbles up everything and retains it. I knew card players who earned their livings from careful observation, impeccable information storage, and judicious play. I couldn't imagine anything more tedious.

"You're kidding," I'd reply to my financial advisers, "that would be a job. I don't want to think. I don't want to communicate. I just want to be surprised. And I want to be left alone!"

I knew full well even then that the casino marketing departments had captured my brain, a brain that was susceptible to external control, a brain that once triggered was almost completely out of control. I didn't care. I'd found an escape and amusement that required no thinking. All it wanted was my money.

As I've been dissecting my disastrous and too-often-delightful years of gambling, I've seen more clearly the threads of manipulation that were woven into an alluring and almost-inescapable snare: the vivid iconic postcard; the easy in and mazelike out of the driveways and parking lots; the gleaming PT Cruiser; the shining smoked glass doors; The Carpet; the design of the slot floors with the machines arranged in cozy groupings; the absence of clocks and windows; the gusts of air-conditioning wafting over my weary face; the old time rock 'n' roll; the buzzers and bells; the attentive staff who remember names of their customers and just happen to show up with a free drink or meal or play voucher just when the gambler is about to quit; the cheap and easy in-and-out buffets; the ATMs that allow busted players to override their daily withdrawal limit; the scent of the air; the "free" rooms, "free" meals, "free" Beanie Babies, commemorative mugs and T-shirts and jackets and hats.

The threads that drew me in and tethered me were—as they might say on Planet Casino—chump change compared to the perks the whales are given: $4–5 million lines of credit for one weekend; bodyguards; luxury dining and private villas with butlers and maids; jet flights; booty bags full of high-quality jewelry, toiletries, watches, tickets to top-drawer shows, and more; and huge loss rebates! The comps and illusions, though rat-size, exerted a powerful hold on a woman who has always found surprises far more rewarding than guarantees.

And then, beyond casino design and promotion, there are the slot machines themselves. To move from the strategies of creating casinos into the programming of the slot machines is to leave behind relatively simple manipulations and enter into designs as elegant and irresistible as the crystalline structure of cocaine. The gambling industry hires sophisticated computer experts to put together reward programs that make B. F. Skinner look like a novice. While the odds for payout are controlled by each state's gambling commission, the programming of the payout deliveries is not.

"Take the player down to extinction." All compulsive slot players might do well to memorize that phrase. They should write it on a card and carry it in their wallet next to their credit cards. It is the gambling industry's goal, and it involves setting up the machines so that gamblers play till their last penny is gone.

How the computer programmers hand the casinos our heads on a pixel platter is a triumph of operant conditioning, computer graphics, and research into the varied minds of compulsive gamblers. In May 2004, *The New York Times* published an article by Gary Rivlin that delineates the ethics, motivations, and sophisticated equipment of International Game Technology of Reno, America's biggest maker of slot machines. Rivlin wrote that "Manufacturers design games primarily for women over 55 with lots of time and disposable income." He spoke with IGT's chief game designer, Anthony Baerlocher, taking us inside a Reno casino.

Baerlocher watched a woman dressed in green polyester pants and a yellow-and-white-striped short-sleeved top play a slot machine he designed called "The Price Is Right." At first, the woman's body language was noncommittal: she stood half-turned from the game, as if no more than mildly curious about the outcome of her wager. "Price" is what slot pros call "a cherry dribbler," a machine that dispenses lots of small payouts while it nibbles at your stash rather than biting off large chunks of it. "You want to give the newbie lots of positive reinforcement—to keep 'em playing," Baerlocher told me. As if on cue, the woman hit a couple of small jackpots and took a seat. "Gotcha," Baerlocher said softly under his breath.

The gaming industry's opportunities for "Gotcha" are being multiplied. Keno and video poker slot machines have existed for years, but now there are setups with a central screen and individual player slots arranged around it that allow players to play blackjack and poker with a virtual dealer—faster and without having to deal with conversation or embarrassment at a losing bet.

Cherry dribblers; machines that hold way back until they deliver a jackpot; machines that give the player free bonus rounds during which wins are doubled, tripled, quadrupled, and more; machines with graphics based on popular television shows; machines with mystical symbols—all of these ultimately lead to Baerlocher's "Gotcha." And the quicker the "Gotcha," the bigger the profits for the casino.

Speed is paramount. The faster a gambler can bet, see the results, and bet again, the faster the brain chemistry is driven. When I first began gambling, part of the ritual was buying rolls of nickels, quarters, and dollars from the cashier. I'd settle in at a machine—not a video machine, but a three-reel mechanical machine—and drop my coins into the slot. I remember my impatience at how slow it was. My MO on those early gambling trips was $20 in nickels, $20 in quarters, $20 in silver dollars. When my 60 bucks was gone, I was done. It was fun, but it was not intoxicating. Plus, I was in it for a win, not for how I felt while I was playing.

A few years later, I began to find machines with paper bill acceptors and video screens. I loved them. I could bet faster. Cashing out was still unwieldy. Though everywhere I played used payout attendants for any amount over $200, I'd often stagger to the cashier balancing three or four buckets of nickels. As my long evenings wore on, the trip became more and more difficult. I'd look at players thirty years my senior and wonder how they did it.

Then the casinos began to pay in paper slips—which could either be cashed out or be fed directly back into the same machine or a new machine. My ritual shifted from rolls of coins to buckets of coins to amassing payout slips in my Holy Fanny Pack, telling myself I would cash them out, take a break, eat a meal, and decide what to do next—but often instead promptly shoving them right back into my machine. What had been a game with which I might earn money had become a trancelike preoccupation in which perpetuating the trance was reward enough.

It would be partially redemptive if I could say now that I am furious about how the casinos "controlled" me, if I could muster moral outrage, if I wanted vengeance. But I don't have that luxury. I'm a classic addict, and I know it. The postcards, the neon, the comps and perks, the slot club attendant arriving just as I was about to cash out because the casino computers were tracking my play—all of that adds up to about 10 percent of why I became a full-tilt gambling addict. Brain chemistry and the unwillingness to grow up account for the other 90 percent. Nobody ever held a gun to my head to force me to walk through those smoked glass doors.

Nonetheless, I am furious when I think about the heartsick women I've met in Scheherazade's Sisters and at casinos, the women I correspond with in my online support group, the women at a local Flagstaff assisted living facility who were thrilled to be bused once a month to Mystic Mesa, where they lost every penny of their Social Security checks. If vengeance is possible for them, I hope this book is part of it.

And, if knowledge is power, I hope to offer to casino workers a few weapons in their struggles for a fair workplace. I've witnessed the gambling corporations' heartless disregard for too many of the casino workers I've met: dealers fired because they had the temerity to age, coin refill attendants and payout employees terminated because it is more profitable for casinos to install paper cashout systems in their slot machines, cashiers timed in their interactions with customers and penalized if they took too long.

Of course, those conditions occur in most corporate workplaces, especially at the level of the actual service providers. When I first moved to the Mojave, I found a chain supermarket where the checkout clerks were the friendliest I'd ever met. Now, I've begun to notice that the clerks are becoming more and more jittery. Our exchanges are short and to the point. One day I see two of the women who used to be friendly taking a break at a local coffee shop. I ask them if I've offended them.

Carla pats the chair next to her. "Sit down," she says. "And you never heard this from us. About three months ago, the bosses started timing how long we took for each transaction. They figured out the maximum time we should spend with each customer. Get the picture?"

I get the picture. Older male casino workers talk consistently about how much better their jobs had been in the days The Boys ran the casinos. More appreciation. More bonuses. The players had known how to tip. As I listen to Carla, it occurs to me that modern American corporations might wield much greater power than the Mob ever had, and that they wield it with equal coldheartedness—and far less grace.

Gambling commissions in Canada, Great Britain, and a few other European countries are exploring (and in some cases initiating) mechanisms that will impose spending and time limits on gambling machine use: allowing a gambler to preset a limit for a day, week, or month and setting up the utilization of "smart cards" that would lock a machine (or machines) after a certain money limit has been reached. The idea behind this is to provide computer monitoring that might allow for intervention.

The Independent Gambling Authority in Australia is considering implementing a program that was tried out in Missouri, in which players were required to swipe an ID card at the entrance to the casino before being allowed in. Predictably, Missouri gamblers stopped playing at local casinos and took their business and compulsion to neighboring states. Missouri removed the card-checking stations and rescinded the loss limitations.

It appears that there is no simple legislative solution for problem gamblers, especially when many states' budgets are linked to legalized lottery play and questions of sovereignty arise specific to Native American casinos. Nonetheless—while the province of this book is not to dive too deeply into resolving the politics and economics of the gambling industry's exploitation of addicted gamblers—it is time for a serious consideration of how much damage is being done.

No matter what is uncovered, I know I will never be off the hook. I will always be a gambling addict. I will always be one bet away from potential mental, physical, and emotional disaster. In the long run, quitting gambling is a personal decision. I and my sister gamblers can take some hope and comfort in the idea that our personal decisions *can* be influenced by education, treatment programs, therapy aimed specifically at gambling addiction, the availability of Gamblers Anonymous—and the weekly support we can find in other support circles like Scheherazade's Sisters.

THE PARTY'S OVER

WHEN IT'S TIME TO STOP

When the Fun Stops . . .

—Problem gambling signs in casinos

There is a second line a woman compulsive gambler may cross—
if she is truly lucky. On one side lies denial of the addiction, on
the other a shock to the nervous system as devastating as a lightning strike. I remember the moment I said to the seven women
gathered around the battered table at a meeting of the Desert
Hot Springs Scheherazade's Sisters: "I have to face it. I really am
addicted to gambling. I've said those words before, but I didn't
truly know."

They all nodded. I recognized that my words must have come
from a place deep inside of me, a place I hadn't visited till that
moment, not even in the Flagstaff Sisters circle or in the six-
month therapy group I'd halfheartedly taken part in. As I spoke,

the room seemed to disappear, and the last five years of my life leaped up in front of me. I saw a bitter, dissatisfied, detached, and lonely woman, a woman who felt calm and whole and fully herself only in the hours between the moment she decided to gamble, pushed through the smoked glass doors into the glorious rainbow glitter and racket, and played "her" slot machines and the time, usually a day or so later, when the drug finally wore off and she returned to a dead zone in her mind and heart.

Between gambling runs, I found the most delicious food tasteless, the most exciting news about my work a weary con, my friends boring. And men? I had been a powerful woman, always on the lookout for a man my equal. But in those last years of gambling, I had found myself saying to any attractive man who sat down and tried to talk to me, "Hey, pal. I'm here to play, not to talk."

The future had become a tedious drone. Until the next moment when I'd find myself thinking, *Hey, I've worked hard on the new novel. I'm going to take myself down the hill to play a few bucks.* From that moment on, everything—putting gas in the car, setting an iced coffee in the beverage holder, taking $200 out of the bank and changing it into fives, driving down I-17 past piñon juniper and glowing red rocks—was a gorgeous ritual.

I remember coming out of the flashback and looking around at the other Scheherazade's Sisters. Their faces were calm, their eyes warm. An older woman smiled, "Welcome home," she said. "Now this time, hush up and listen."

I loved our circle. I loved driving down the desert highway knowing I was heading for a room in which impeccable truth would be told and judgment had been parked outside the door. I loved hearing that I was not alone. Perhaps more than anything, I loved hearing our differences and remembering the almost-Buddhist paradox that it was what we had grievously in common that bound us together.

I thought often about our weird luck in, as Delfina once said, "having so much fun gambling I couldn't have fun anymore—anywhere." The stories of how we had bottomed out were as different as our autobiographies, and in many ways they were the same. Casinos post a notice near ATMs and cashiers' cages that reads: WHEN THE FUN STOPS. There is an 800 number for the problem gamblers' hotline. I remember looking at the little sign and thinking, Not for me. Until the fun inevitably did stop—not during the hours I was gambling, but in every other second of my life. Every woman in Scheherazade's Sisters had talked about the moment when she started to wonder where the fun had gone.

We all know stepping over the line onto a slick and irresistible slope, hearing the phantom voice of reality and ignoring it, and finally feeling our knotted hearts unclench as we said, "I can't keep doing this," and finally meaning it. For some Sisters, it was their own awakening, for others, an external door slammed shut. What we all had in common was the knowledge that once we had crossed that second line from denial to awareness, there could never be any turning back. We might gamble again, we might even get hooked, but we would never again believe that we could gamble just for fun.

Barb tells us a story we've heard before—about driving home from the casino after her biggest hit: $10,000 on a dollar machine. She'd managed to hang on to $1,500 of it. It was 2:30 AM. The road blurred in front of her. She slammed the last of the cold coffee in the Burger King cup and wondered whether she should pull over.

Her sister was with the kids, and she had her cell, so she could call. But she didn't have a headset, and she was scared that if she pulled over she'd fall asleep. So she drove on. Smoke from the forest fires in the north hung in the air. She almost welcomed it, as though a soft, gray blanket were holding her and her car.

Barb pulled off the highway onto the main road that led to her street. She turned the corner and saw red and blue lights flashing in front of her house. "I nearly drove into a telephone pole. I knew it was the baby. I knew she was dead. Something had happened that my sister couldn't handle. And if she was dead, I had killed her."

Two cop cars were parked on the street. Barb drove into her garage and forced herself to walk out to where they were parked. A tall officer unfolded himself from the passenger seat and walked up to her. "Please show me your driver's license," he said. Barb couldn't move.

"My baby," she said. "What happened?"

For an instant, his face was soft. "Your baby's fine, ma'am. Please let me see your ID."

An hour later, Barb stood face to face with a booking officer. She was too numb from shock and eighteen hours on the same dollar slot to feel anything. "We are booking you for embezzlement," the officer said. "Officer Ronald will read you your Miranda rights, and then you may make a call to your lawyer. If you don't have one, we can contact the public defender."

"I swear to god," Barb tells us, "my first thought was, *The jig is up*. My second thought was, *I wish I'd played out that last fifteen hundred*. And now I know that even then I hadn't faced the fact that I was never going to be able to gamble again without major consequence. It took a year or so of court-ordered counseling and being with all of you for me to catch on."

Each of us has told the circle our story of the moment we'd never wanted to face. Sometimes we repeat it for the sake of anchoring those most powerful moments. I have often wondered why my realizations have been relatively easy by comparison. Delfina tells us of waking slowly from a long, strange dream to find her husband looking down at her and saying, "*Vieja, amor*, wake up. I have called the priest and an ambulance. Tell me why you have done this."

"My mouth didn't work very well. I tried a few times and finally said, 'But what have I done?' He patted my hand and said we would talk later. The ambulance and the priest came. Only after they treated me at the hospital and the priest sent my husband from the room so he and I could talk alone did I remember what I had done. And then I wished I hadn't woken up.

"I'd forged a prescription for sleeping pills. I'd taken all of them. It had seemed very simple. I would just be gone. There would be no pending mortgage foreclosure, no credit company threats, no bills opened and shredded. I just would go to sleep. I would deal with God when I came to him. But then there was a rosy glow behind my eyelids and my husband's voice reaching me as if from far, far away."

She laughs. "Did I decide to stop that minute? Oh no. It took six months with my husband watching me with his eagle eye, so I would come straight home from work and stay in all night, before my brain got clear enough for me to know I *had* to be finished. That was an awful moment. And then I battled depression for a year or so until I found all of you."

As I listen to Delfina, I remember how Candace had a suicide attempt as well. There was only one time my gambling edged me into feeling suicidal. Feeling. Only feeling. I've known since my first deep panic attack when I was twelve that suicide would never be a doorway for me. My mother had been hospitalized for suicidal psychotic depression. "Your mom's gone to the hospital again," was all my father said to my younger brother and me. He prided himself on being a man of few words. I know now how terrified he must have been, and how angry. It was 1952, and my mother's psychiatrists informed them that her depression was a ploy to get attention and to punish.

That night I lay in my bed fighting sleep. For years I'd been frightened that I, too, would succumb to that condition of no control that possessed my mother. Suddenly, I thought, *I am going to die someday*. I felt a terrible nothingness begin to spread out from my heart. *Everybody dies. You will not escape death. Someday, you will not be.* I felt myself launched into cold, black space. Lights flashed past me. I was conscious. I was alone. And all those conditions were eternal.

I jolted out of bed, ran down the stairs, and found my father on the couch reading *Time* magazine. "Daddy," I said, "I'm going to die someday."

He looked at me. "Oh, that won't be for a long time." He didn't put his arm around me. He turned back to his reading.

I wondered if he'd heard me. "No, Daddy, I mean someday I'll be dead."

He put down his magazine. "You know, Mary Liz, the priests tell us about this. We don't have to be afraid. We'll be with God." Again he turned back to his reading.

I sat frozen. I knew, in that instant, that my father was not a powerful being who could make everything right. He was a cardboard cutout, as was the priest. And I was alone with my knowledge. And terrified of dying.

Through decades of severe depression, too many seductive and unavailable men, too many bad choices, I'd never considered killing myself, with the possible exception of a time when I tried an antidepressant and found myself having weird, unemotional thoughts about how easy suicide might be. Gin, work, reading, compulsively taking care of other people, food, shopping, throwing myself into causes—I took on anything that dulled the pain. But *end* the pain? To find myself drifting brutally alone forever? Not possible. I couldn't imagine what wanting to kill oneself would feel like.

Until I found myself on an icy October 3:00 AM in 2000 trudging to my hotel room from the casinos in Deadwood, South Dakota. I loathed myself in a way I'd never experienced. I couldn't imagine why I would want to wake up the next morning.

A ferocious plains ice storm had closed down my writing residency at Bear Lodge (Devils Tower) a day earlier. I-90 to the west was closed. I could have stayed overnight with one of the park rangers and taken off the next midday for Flagstaff. Instead I remembered that Deadwood was not too far away. I'd always wanted to visit the town, an old gold-mining city that had converted to gambling in 1989. I checked the map. Forty-three easy miles. I was on the road. I had 60 bucks in my wallet. Life was at its sweetest.

I drove into Deadwood and was enchanted. The town had converted its old downtown stores and businesses into casinos. The streets were a time machine into the late 1800s. I rented a hotel room and walked out into the crisp air and glittering lights. I was perhaps one of a few hundred customers in the town. The highway closure had resulted in my having my own personal casinos.

I loved gambling in privacy. I adored driving down to Mystic Mesa at 6:30 in the morning and walking into a near-empty casino. When my former gambling pal, Everett, and I went together, we would open the entrance doors, suck in a deep breath of the air, turn to each other, and say (à la Colonel Kilgore in *Apocalypse Now*), "I love the smell of an empty casino in the morning."

I walked into the first neon-jeweled storefront in Deadwood and found my new favorite slot machine. I played for an hour or so and walked out up $150. I kept going. The next casino forked over $200, the next a $300 hand-pay. I took a break in a hokey mountain man restaurant and tried Rocky Mountain oysters for the first time. They were a disappointment, but for the next three hours they were Deadwood's only disappointment.

I rocketed to an $800 profit on my $60 investment. By 1:00 AM it occurred to me that since I had to drive home the next morning, I might want to take my fat wallet back to the hotel room. But there was one more near-empty casino.

Me being me, and the casinos being the casinos, I had to check it out. I lost 50 bucks, then 100. I knew the feeling in my gut. It was the chilly foreboding hardcore gamblers feel when they know their luck has turned. I lost another 200 and started chasing my losses, staying in one casino, making bigger and bigger bets, moving from one machine to another, finally stubbornly settling in at a machine that went from lukewarm to chilly to dry ice.

I counted my stash: $250. I forced myself to get up and drag myself away from the iceberg, out the door, and up the street to the hotel. I talked to myself all the way to my room. "You know better. You could have walked home with a $800 profit. *And* you've got a room reserved at the Gold Dust Motel in Blackhawk (a Colorado gambling town) tomorrow night. You'll have the chance to gamble again. You fucked up. Big time."

I felt as though I had swallowed acid. My whole being concentrated around a huge and necrotic disappointment. A disappointment not with Deadwood, but with myself. I was desperate to not occupy my body. I remembered being in a protracted labor with one of my kids and wishing I could take my head and mind off my body, set them on a shelf, and return for them when the baby was finally born. This was worse.

I got myself back into my room, ate a few crackers I'd filched from the mountain man restaurant figuring that would help my blood sugar, and crawled into bed. I lay awake for hours, trapped in a litany of blame and despair. I finally understood why some people try to kill themselves.

Dawn came far too early. I woke, looked over at the $250 on the bed stand, and tried to New Age psychobabble myself into a state of optimism. "It's a learning experience. Be grateful for what the Universe gives you. Let go. Let go." All I wanted to let go of was my brain. I made coffee, slammed it down, and got the hell out of Deadwood as fast as I could.

I don't fully understand why that particular episode took me down to bone and marrow, down to an understanding of my mother I had never had. Ingratitude comes to mind. A lifelong inability to feel happiness for longer than a few hours comes to mind. Sheer brain chemistry may be the answer—because eight hours later I was cheerfully hunkered down on one of the upstairs Cleopatra slot machines in the Mardi Gras Casino in Blackhawk, Colorado, with no memory of the horror I'd felt.

Barb and Delfina had both been dragged by devastating choices into quitting. Helen had been dragged by her family. She came home after a three-day binge to find her husband, daughters, grandson, and a stranger in her living room. The family had worked with a counselor at a gambling treatment center to design and carry out an intervention. "I wanted to kill every one of them," she tells us. "They sent me to a treatment program. I was the only gambler. Everybody else was young and on drugs or alcohol—or both. I did what the counselors told me to do, shut my mouth unless I was asked to talk, and got out of there with no intention of quitting.

"It took over a year for me to finally stop. Finally, my husband took all my credit cards and kept all our money. He went shopping with me. He went everywhere with me. Maybe that was enough for me to finally promise him I'd quit! Now, from sitting here with you girls, I know in my mind that I can't make another bet." She laughs. "But every time we drive by a casino, my fingers get itchy. You know."

The stories continue. K-Siu's almost-killing shame the night her husband left and she was alone looking at the empty spaces where her family heirlooms had once rested. Sharon's sorrow when she walked out of the casino into what she knew was a gorgeous morning and couldn't hear the birds, see dawn as anything but a blur, smell the sweet desert morning air. Nora's terror when Jen sat her down at their computer and walked her through their online bank accounts. "And even then," she says, "it took me two years of coming to this circle before I could cut up my slot cards."

Ginny listens quietly through much of our sharing and reminiscing. It isn't till after our break that she says, "I don't know if I've crossed the line. I think of gambling all the time."

Tiffany nods, "Me, too."

"It's different for different people," Nora says. "We talk a lot in Narcotics Anonymous about hitting bottom. Going back out to use is most common for gamblers over all other addicts. It's that euphoric recall business, all those sparkly memories I'm probably going to carry to my grave."

I feel grateful—for once in my life—to feel normal, to feel part of a group. I think about how fast slot machine addiction can seize a gambler—in two years max, rather than the ten to fifteen years it takes an action player to get hooked. All of us in the circle were in trouble within a few years. All of us in the circle bottomed out on slots. While Candace and K-Siu had also been action players, by the time they were dangerously hooked, they were on slots. Not one of us has ever said that the thought of gambling disgusts us. Indeed, though we are shaken by our memories of how deeply hooked we were, *and* the consequences of our gambling—marriages and homes lost, financial ruin, bankruptcy, precious family ties damaged or severed—we still live with the "sparkly" memories and urges more often than we might like.

Perhaps that is the power of euphoric recall specific to slot addiction. Perhaps we are unusual in our lack of disgust. I've read books and websites by women gambling addicts who do feel horror at the thought of gambling. Women Helping Women (www .femalegamblers.info) is a powerful monthly newsletter organized by Marilyn Lancelot, author of *Gripped by Gambling*, her true story of finding herself being taken away to jail in her early sixties because of her compulsive gambling.

The website is filled with stories written by women gambling addicts both caught in and free from their compulsive behaviors. Their voices are raw and immediate:

Thinking back, I remember teaching little kids in church. Being so close to God, I felt his presence all the time. Now I don't feel his presence, and when I pray it is like no one is home. I do not want to die being an active addicted gambler.

My son Eddie was home visiting for three weeks, and once he left I experienced such an overbearing sense of loneliness. We also learned Christine is back in the hospital after a third suicide attempt, and even if I went back to New Jersey, the psych unit she is on doesn't permit visitors. I ran to the casino and hid there until the money ran out and the shame set in. . . .

I can't speak for the other women in Scheherazade's Sisters. Each woman's story is her own. Each woman is a unique bundle of history, emotions, and longings. My passage from active addiction to always-temporary remission perhaps only seems relatively easy based on what I imagine other scenarios would have felt like. But perhaps other women in the circle feel they had it easy compared to me.

I look back on the events that pushed me over the line—*pushed me*. I have never felt that I crossed by my own volition. I hadn't run out of money. By hook or by crook, through grace, hustling, and endless years of hard work, by gritty miracles, shameless cons, and the extraordinary and nonjudgmental generosity of friends, I have had a home, food, and a vehicle since I was a homeless hippie in the early '60s. I wasn't dead broke, institutionalized, or locked up in jail. Nobody sat me down, looked me in the eye, and said, "I'm leaving you if you don't quit." My denial was ironclad—in the face of the Flagstaff Scheherazade's Sisters and six months of outpatient gambling treatment.

My body pushed me over the line.

I'm not a religious woman. I've known for years that any thought system that teaches that body and spirit are at best separate, and at worst at war, is a danger to the human heart. I've been taught that personal wisdom by the joy of making love, the beauty of the natural world, and the powerful intelligence of my dreams. And once I began to understand that despite our best efforts, the wisdom of the body cannot, in the long run, be overruled, I learned to imperfectly listen to what my body told me.

I tried to outrun its messages. I ate when my full stomach cramped. I drank booze when I could barely move my lips to speak. I stayed with lovers when my guts were twisted into knots. I sat on slot machine stools while my legs went numb and my blood sugar plummeted until I almost fell over. I worked twelve-hour days while my body whimpered, "I have to lie down."

Then, in 1988, I skipped breakfast; wrote till midafternoon; ran to Macy's, a Flagstaff coffee shop; bolted down a brownie and double house coffee; and raced off to run errands. I was in the post office line when I realized I was having trouble seeing. There was a blind spot in my left eye. The edges of the spot began to shimmer like rainbows. The rainbows and the spot spread through my entire left visual field. I waited to drop dead. But the postal clerk called my name, so I stepped up to the counter.

The postal worker seemed to be speaking a blend of English and Sanskrit. I could see enough out of my right eye to interpret what she was saying. I gave her my packages, paid for the postage, and left. I sat on the low stone wall outside the post office. I was thoroughly opposed to dying—after all, my material self was as holy as my soul. I didn't have a cell phone. I wasn't going to embarrass myself by grabbing a perfect stranger and saying, "Hey, could you help me? I'm having a stroke." I waited.

The rainbow aura grew, then seemed to drift off the edges of my visual field. My head ached. My thoughts seemed garbled, but I knew I was hyperventilating, so I walked to my car and drove home. My doctor called me back an hour after I'd called. It was, after all, the late '80s. She told me I'd most likely had an ophthalmic migraine, that I should watch for more and come in for a pamphlet on the condition. I drove to her office and picked up the pamphlet.

I learned that ophthalmic migraines are unruly and mysterious. While they are caused by constriction of blood vessels to the brain, none of the experts know exactly what causes them. The triggers are many: food allergy; stress; changes in barometric pressure, temperature, posture, and altitude; low blood sugar; and more. Chocolate, MSG, nitrates, and white grape juice are primary culprits. Ophthalmic migraines are almost impossible to abort, and medications don't always control them—and have hellacious side effects.

I put down the pamphlet, walked into the kitchen, and took four Cadbury bars, a bag of Oreos, a pint of chocolate ice cream, and a box of Droste cocoa mix from my cupboard. I carried them to a friend's house. She looked at me. "Are you nuts? What about PMS?"

"Migraines are worse," I said. "I'm allergic to chocolate."

I never had another migraine until January 3, 2008. I was forty miles from Flagstaff on I-40, returning from a cross-country solo road trip to visit my daughter and family in North Carolina. I'd taken a break at the little Acoma casino just outside Albuquerque, played a few bucks (down $300, till the last machine spit out $325), and eaten the suspiciously flavorful buffet. The gas gauge warning light shone. I pulled off in Winslow to buy gas.

As I put my credit card in the pump reader, I saw a familiar wavering spot in my vision. "The buffet," I thought. "MSG." I drove the last miles to Flagstaff through the shimmering aura, popped an Advil when I got home, and promised myself to be more careful with what I ate.

A week later, there was another migraine. Then two in one day. I couldn't spot a food trigger. I drove to Twentynine Palms to teach a writing workshop and give a benefit reading for the Mojave Desert Land Trust. I was careful about road food, but just past Amboy I drove toward the setting sun for fifteen minutes and saw the blind patch begin.

It was that spring when I decided to move to Twentynine Palms. The migraines continued, intensified in frequency, and left me terrified on top of being frightened about the changes I was wreaking in my life. The day I moved to Twentynine Palms, the sunset-triggered migraine reoccurred. I drove down the long slope of Iron Mountain toward Twentynine Palms, and despite the usual brain garble in my mind, I thought, *Maybe gambling has something to do with the migraines*.

The migraines increased in frequency, one a day, two a day. I was past figuring out what caused them. I'd Googled everything I could find and come away with the same information in the pamphlet I'd read in 1988. I went to a local doctor who listened for two minutes, offered me medication, and then said, "Well, if not for the migraines, perhaps something for your anxiety."

There seemed to be nowhere to turn. I knew no one in Twentynine Palms. Flagstaff seemed light years away. I made it through one more night in my tiny homestead cabin, woke in the full grip of the damnable rainbow aura, and knew I needed, if not help, at least a few people I could talk honestly with.

I called Donna, she called a friend, and I found honest women and help.

I had my last ophthalmic migraine in January 2008. I gambled once between January 3, 2007, and now. I have no idea how those two blessings are linked. I suspect they may, indeed, be blessings. But I am not a religious woman, so I have to leave it to mystery. I leave it to hitting a wall I didn't know existed. Now I believe that only in hitting that wall can I or any true gambling addict find hope.

A LONG AND WINDING ROAD

WITHDRAWAL

*You mean just stop? Cold turkey? You don't understand! The
pain . . .*

—Frankie Machine in *The Man with the Golden Arm*, 1955

I looked over at Everett. His jaw was set. He hung on to the steering wheel as though it were a life preserver. "We are getting out of here," he said. "Now."

Now was January 1, 2002. We were in Ev's old truck in the parking lot of a Nevada casino. It was just past dawn. The jittering neon of the huge signs seemed washed-out. I held a free coffee mug in my hand that had cost me $480. Everett looked back at me. "I don't know. Maybe it's time to quit."

He pulled out onto the main street. I chugged my watery coffee. Ev grinned. "Is that helping any?" I laughed. "Graveyard humor," he said. It was an old joke we'd heard in a defunct little Native American casino north of the Arizona strip, something about two skeletons playing blackjack side by side—one of them says, "This dealer is killing me."

"Yeah," I said, "you just heard the laugh of a woman about to go through who-knows-how-long gambling withdrawal—at the same time she's on deadline for a book she has no idea how to write."

"Maybe we ought to check out that free gambling addiction counseling program at the hospital," he suggested.

A week later, we found ourselves in a conference room with one-way observation windows and a long table. We sat with a sad-looking woman, a tiny man in a plaid sport coat, and a sweet-faced shrink. "Welcome," the shrink said, "welcome to the new part of your life." His voice was kind. Ev winced. I tried to smile. We'd both been through decades of therapy and recovery. I moonlighted as a counselor. It was unsettling hearing the guy say the same words I'd so often said to my clients.

The therapy group was free, as was a weekly counseling session with a different psychologist whose heart was as generous as his big brain. Arizona Native American casinos funded them. The group was based on the Gamblers Anonymous model, though it was not a GA group. We worked with basic GA principles and wrote out the twelve steps.

At first I took my quitting seriously. I listened to the other gamblers. The first step was easy. I knew I was powerless over the addiction. I had a harder time with the second step, which required me to come to believe that a Power greater than myself could "restore me to a normal way of thinking and living." I don't question that there is much in this vast universe that is greater than me, but I wasn't sure I wanted to be restored to normalcy. Plus I wasn't sure I was capable of letting that happen. I've taken pride in not being normal since I was in junior high and realized that what I had thought was a curse in my childhood was what made me "me."

The third step, which reads: "Made a decision to turn our will and our lives over to the care of this Power of our own understanding," stopped me cold. My Catholic girlhood reared up and smacked me. G-d was not interested in anyone having fun. G-d put humans through impossible paces so they could prove themselves worthy of "His" "love." G-d would turn me into a pious robot. And I knew that if I took this step, I'd have to give up gambling forever.

GA teaches that "forever" cannot exist for the true addict. Recovery can only be managed a day at a time. But I am an addict and therefore grandiose and catastrophic, so it was impossible to not leap into the dreadful, dull future that seemed to stretch out ahead of me—no matter how loving some hypothetical higher power might be.

I surfed steps 2 and 3 and dove into step 4. I "made a searching and fearless moral and financial inventory" of myself. I read it to the group. And, for the first three months it took to do those steps, I didn't gamble. Ev, too, stayed clean. He may have even read his fourth step to the group. I can't remember. I was in a haze of withdrawal, compounded by the disassociation I go through writing anything I am not possessed by. I forced myself through my days. There was no room in my brain to store any memories.

I'd wake at five, try to go back to sleep, and make myself lie still while my mind rattled through a dozen fatal illnesses and annihilating mental disorders. I'd give up around five thirty, drag myself from bed, light a fire in the icy woodstove, drink a huge mug of strong coffee, eat just enough for fuel, and slump into the chair at my writing desk. I'd open up the computer and stare into the gray screen. My mind felt even grayer. All I wanted to do was go back to bed, but I knew that would be not comfort, but rather torment. I opened up the book I was working on. It had no name. For those first three months of my withdrawal, it had no form or heart.

In August 2001, I'd signed on for three books with a New York publisher: a novel, *Going Through Ghosts;* an already-written short story collection called *Delicate;* and an untitled memoir of a year of being offline. The editor and I had envisioned the third book as a collection of essays drawn from journal entries I'd kept in 2000. We were inspired by listeners' reactions to a "going offline" commentary I'd read on NPR in February 2001—people talked about being lonelier with email than without, wishing they weren't dependent on it, and, in the most poignant message from a woman, wishing she could live her values.

The memoir would be filled with true stories of paddling on wild Western rivers, sitting for hours on my peaceful back deck with only the company of ravens and light, writing real letters on real paper to people who wrote back their joy that they knew we would hold each others' words in our hands. I would trace my journey back from pixels to a multidimensional sensual life. I would write about how slowing down from cyber speed to cellular speed would take patience and no small amount of moving through the discomfort of unhooking. I'd quit email and the Internet because I had become addicted to them.

Then, a month after I signed the contract, two planes smashed into the World Trade Center, one into the Pentagon, and another into a field in Pennsylvania. I called my editor two days later and said, "I have to write a different book. The time for deeply introspective and charming essays by women lucky enough to change their lives is over. This book has to be one of the threads that readers can use as tethers to something."

"Yes," she said. "But tethers to what?"

"I don't know," I said. "That's the point."

It had taken me four months to begin to approach the new book. I dug through my journals from 2000. That time seemed centuries gone. I missed who I'd been, what my life had been, what America had seemed to be. Finally, in January 2002, a week after I stopped gambling, I knew it was time to begin writing. It was the last thing I wanted to do.

I'd gone back online. There's no way to be a working writer in America without Internet access to agents, publishers, bookstores, and research. As I stared at what seemed to be runes on the computer screen in front of me, I forced myself again and again not to check my email. Heat would begin to spread through my body. I'd sweat as though I were in a sauna rather than a drafty cabin during a mountain February. My thoughts bounced off each other. No two sentences in my mind fell into a sequence. I was sixty-two, long past hot flashes and long past the squirrely chittering of my brain that had tormented most of my passage through menopause. I was sure I'd begun the descent into either fatal leukemia or Alzheimer's.

I slogged on. I was used to mild discomfort when I was in full writing mode. I always teach my students that it is almost impossible to write at one's best without plenty of nothing around the actual writing. That is most true for me when I'm working on a long essay or novel. I am, after all, an addict. Addicts hate *nothing*. We will do anything to escape the emptiness that is at the bottom of an aware human consciousness. Every time I opened up the document of the book that had no name, I opened up the door into my emptiness.

Ev showed up one morning when I was pacing my living room. "I'm going crazy," I said. "I can't think. I bet I have leukemia. I can't stop sweating, and I have no appetite, and there are lumps in my lymph nodes, and all I want to do is sleep, and I can't think. I know! My leukemia went into my brain, and I have a fatal tumor that is going to drive me crazy before I die."

Ev picked up my giant coffee mug and tapped the side. "Not too much of this?" he said. I wanted to smack him. On top of going crazy, having leukemia, and descending into Alzheimer's, *everything* pissed me off.

"Has it occurred to you," he said mildly, "that you are in intense gambling withdrawal and writing a book you don't know how to write?"

"Oh," I said.

"Look," he said, "why don't you Google 'gambling withdrawal' and find out what the symptoms are?" He paused and looked me hard in the eyes. "But no matter what's going on, you still have to write the book."

He pulled up a chair. I typed "gambling withdrawal" into Google search and hit return. There was nothing. "How can that be?" Ev said. "I don't know," I said. We kept hunting, trying different terms. All we could find were a few gambling support sites, Gamblers Anonymous, and a galaxy of opportunities to gamble online. "This is crazy," I said.

"Call the gambling hotline," he told me.

"I have. It's this old guy who just tells me to sit on my hands."

"Call them again."

I called. A woman answered the phone. "Hey, I'm Dee Dee. How can I help you?" I told her what I was going through. In one sentence, she tossed me a lifeline. "Honey, your brain is metabolizing overtime. You're kicking out chemical like crazy." She gave me another number to call. "There's a woman who went through exactly what you're going through. Her name is Carlotta, and she works at home, so she'll be there."

I thanked Dee Dee, hung up, and dialed the number. An answering machine picked up. I left a message and sat with my hands in my lap. I ignored the irony that I was doing exactly what the old guy had kept telling me to do.

Ev headed for the kitchen. "I'm going to make breakfast."

"I can't eat."

"Who said anything about *your* breakfast?"

"Thanks," I said, "for the pep talk."

The phone rang. "Is Mary there?" The woman's voice was husky. I heard years of cigarettes and booze in it. "I am Mary," I said.

"I'm Carlotta. Dee Dee said you could use a little fellowship. I'm not a gambler, but I'm fifteen years sober in AA. What's going on?"

My thoughts lurched. "I can't think," I said. "I mean I'm two months clean from gambling, and my brain feels like it's broken."

"Oh, sweetheart," she said. "You know they don't tell us enough about this part of getting clean. I think it goes back to old AA, when the boys had to be tough and not talk about feelings.

"Let me tell you, girlfriend, remembering that part of withdrawal is sometimes the only thing that keeps me sober. I was sure I was going crazy. I couldn't afford therapy, so AA meetings were my only help. They kept me on the planet until maybe my brain finally healed a little. It'll never be normal. I know that. But when I could put two thoughts together and then find a third, I felt like a woman dying of thirst who had just swallowed clean water. And then I heard another woman in my women's meeting say that during the first months of her recovery, her brain felt like it was neurotransmitter soup."

I felt my hand relax on the phone. "You're breathing," Carlotta said, "I just heard you take a deep breath. Keep doing that. Those long, slow breaths. You do that short, fast breathing; you hyperventilate; and it makes you feel even crazier. I learned that in my women's group, too."

"Okay," I said. "I'm not crazy, but there aren't any GA meetings up here. I've got to find some other women to talk with. We had a circle, not GA, but it died out. And I haven't got the brain or time to start a new one."

"I'll make some calls," Carlotta said. "You know you can call me and Dee Dee any time you want."

We said goodbye. I felt a little relief, but mostly I wanted to cry. Ev called out from the kitchen. "Did they help?"

"A little. But I've got to find more than just the therapy group to talk to. I need to get down and dirty."

"Google 'women gamblers,'" Ev said. "That might be a place to start."

I did. Women Helping Women flashed up on the screen. Marilyn Lancelot had been writing about gambling addiction since 1999. She wrote about her harrowing descent into compulsive slot gambling, and she published stories from other women gambling addicts, some still hooked, some managing to stay clean.

I read story after story. As I did, my thoughts began to clear a little, though I found few references to withdrawal. Nonetheless, I was happy to feel a little less alone. I decided to write Marilyn and ask her to post my experience.

I wrote my message as fast as my fingers could move. In some ways, it was the real beginning of the book I'd been wrestling with, the book that became the memoir/meditation/rant titled *Solace: Rituals of Loss and Desire.* Everett cooked breakfast, and I wrote this:

I work as a writer. My brain and hands are my tools, for earning a living and for journal writing through the challenges of being a sixty-two-year-old single woman with intense mood swings—who cannot take medication.

I owe what little serenity I have this morning, fifty-six days since my last slot bet, to my gambling therapy group—and to Mario Puzo. He wrote in the mid-'70s, " . . . I had to give up gambling at a certain period in my life because I found I could no longer write if I continued gambling."

Seven years of increasingly intense binge gambling left me deep in debt—not only to credit cards, but to my brain. At first, playing slots was pure fun, the casinos a playground for a woman who never had a childhood, who spent decades taking care of other people. I began to only feel normal in the casinos. My "other" time was spent in irritability and tension. I wrote less and less.

I had quit drinking years before. That was easy. My first few days of gambling withdrawal were fine. I knew I was still in the drugged state. Then, fear kicked in. I started to notice every ache in my body, every second of heartburn or breathlessness. I became convinced I had a fatal illness.

As I moved through that fear, a worse obsession kicked in. I monitored my every thought, became terrified I was going into Alzheimer's, or insanity. I couldn't read, my comfort since childhood. I wanted to get compulsively busy, which has always blocked fear in the past. And, I couldn't lose myself in busyness.

I am writing a book. Time is essential. I couldn't give it away to workaholism. I made myself go slow.

I went to my therapy group, read Gamblers Anonymous literature and anything else I could find—and couldn't find anything about feeling crazy during withdrawal. I doubted my sanity even more. So, I walked and talked to What Might Be Bigger Than Me and listened to a best friend who said, "I think you're just in process." I trusted—barely—and lived a minute at a time—barely.

I yelled at my Higher Power—who often seems like a cross between Tina Turner and George Carlin.

Then, I called the Arizona gambling hotline and lucked into a wonderful counselor named Dee Dee, who said, "Honey, your brain is metabolizing overtime. You're kicking out chemical like crazy."

She sent me to another woman who said that the first weeks of her initial withdrawal from alcohol were like living in "neurotransmitter soup."

. . . If any of you have just quit gambling and think you are going crazy, you're not. Go to meetings, call sober friends, call the national or local hotline. Reread my experience, strength, and hope, and know that you are going sane.

I want to know more.

Ev brought me a plate filled with a feta cheese omelet, fried potatoes with rosemary, and hot toast. I ate. He read what I'd written. "I think it's not as bad for me," he said, "because I have to take a break from the casinos all summer when I'm up in Idaho working in wilderness. You've been at it pretty steady."

I nibbled at the toast. It was the first food that had tasted good in months. "I might live," I said. "But it really pisses me off that there's so little information on withdrawal. It's not enough to tell some addicts to bear with it a day at a time or to keep coming back. Some of us need to know that what we're going through isn't in our imaginations, and also that we're not in real danger."

"You know how addiction recovery programs talk about addiction as a disease that tells us we don't have a disease," Ev said. "What you're going through is a dis-ease that tells you that you do have a disease."

"That's it," I said. "And then I panic. I hyperventilate, and that really feels like going crazy."

We finished our food. He walked back to his place—the cabin next door. I put a log in the woodstove and sat back down to write.

In the week before I found the Desert Hot Springs Scheherazade's Sisters in 2008 and said, "I have to face it. I really am addicted to gambling," I suspected I was in the first stages of withdrawal—trouble sleeping, a lack of pleasure in anything I did, a steady-state jitteriness that could only be relieved by four-mile walks. I fought the creeping in of the obsessive thoughts that I might be descending into Alzheimer's.

I tried again to find information about gambling withdrawal on the Internet. Marilyn Lancelot was still faithfully publishing Women Helping Women. It was chilling—and reassuring—to read other women's stories, but I found so little on withdrawal. I clung to Carlotta's words—"neurotransmitter soup." I contacted a few GA message boards, but nobody was talking about withdrawal. I bought half a dozen books on gambling addiction and found nothing.

The closest I came to the information that would have reassured me that I didn't have dementia was in a site for cocaine addicts. The description of cocaine withdrawal sounded a lot like what I was going through. And it wasn't enough.

The essence of panic—for those of us who are afflicted with it—is that it obliterates the ability to take comfort from past knowledge. No matter what I had learned in earlier withdrawals, the terror that I felt was compounded by the presence of the migraines. They made me feel utterly out of control of my brain, and my brain had been my last line of defense when all else failed. I'd learned that through my mother's psychotic breaks, when reading and thinking had held me together.

I reread GA literature and still found nothing specific to withdrawal. I talked about some of the panic and disassociation I was experiencing in Scheherazade's Sisters, but I held back much. I was terrified that one of them would look at me and say, "That sounds like what happened to my great-aunt." They would stop talking and look away. I would know exactly what had happened to the great-aunt.

One of the primary reasons I came to wanting to write a book about women and gambling was because of the lack of information I was experiencing about withdrawal. It was a relief to find one thing I wanted to do. I was so lost to any pleasure in my life that I had taken to making it through one minute at a time. I wonder now if in that time without plans, without structure, without using, there may have finally been a little room in my mind for inspiration. And then, of course, there was the compelling power of the other Sisters' stories.

I was grateful for a few structured tasks: I dug into books and online information. I learned about dopamine and comorbidity and what happens for compulsive people when they cease their compulsive behavior. A few months later, I walked away from an alluring and potentially disastrous romantic intrigue and plunged into the most severe withdrawal I had ever felt.

Despite days of obsessing about my every thought, days of words breaking up into fragments, a month or more of not being able to read to relax and monitoring for strokes and waking at three in the morning with my brain on automatic horror, I wrote. When I couldn't think clearly enough to work on the book, I wrote scraps of poetry by hand.

I walked for hours in the late afternoon and twilight desert. I found a dead and fallen Joshua tree that looked like a seated Buddha. I found an abandoned house surrounded with dry pools and boulders that once had been placed to make waterfalls. As I approached the house, a flock of white pigeons flew up from the eaves. Later that day, I read a bit of information in the back of my most recent issue of *Audubon* magazine, and I began to suspect that I might be healing in a way I never had before and that there was more at work than my human will. I jotted down the words *White Pigeon Ticket*.

The next morning I woke at five instead of three. I drank peppermint tea—I'd stopped drinking coffee when I'd read that it could be linked to OCD in older coffee junkies—and I said my meditation: *For the furthering of all sentient beings and the protection of earth, air, and water.* I watched the dark along the eastern horizon shift molecule by molecule to silver-gray. As I murmured the final *earth, air, and water,* the words *White Pigeon Ticket* flashed across my mind.

I picked up my journal and wrote:

White Pigeon Ticket

I

White Pigeon Ticket came across
 the ocean,
 the centuries,
  brought by memories
  and stories
  of Chinese laborers in the early American West.

 The game was no longer White Pigeon Ticket,
  but Keno.

II

I rarely played Keno.
The game was too slow
    too tediously noisy.

I played Cleopatra 20-line.
There were bonuses
    three golden pyramids promising
        fifteen free spins
        all wins tripled.
There was jackpot music
    no coins jangled in
        or out.

I slipped a bill into a slot.
The bet was silent.
When the time came to leave
    (the player never wants to leave)
    I pressed Cash Out
    The screen read: Are you sure you want to stop?

There was, say, $42.60 left
of a $600. jackpot
and the $300. I had slid
one twenty at a time
into the slot.
        I was sure.

          Not that I wanted to stop

but that
I had to.
I pressed Cash Out again.
The paper voucher emerged
without a sound.

III

I walked past a bank of keno machines
and an ATM. A woman hunched in close to the ATM.
(She was not me
and she was.)
She slid a credit card
into the machine and stepped back.

INSUFFICIENT FUNDS
another card
INSUFFICIENT FUNDS
Four more cards.
INSUFFICIENT FUNDS
INSUFFICIENT FUNDS
INSUFFICIENT FUNDS
INSUFFICIENT FUNDS

IV

Seven months since my last bet.
My brain is sandpapered.
I walk into the Mojave

I walk alongside a pale rising moon.
    Mountains below the moon
        are deep violet
        and the rich brown of
        elk-hide.

I think of my old home
and how once in a time of deep grief,
    I stepped out my back door
    and watched the elk stag
    watch me
    through dawn mist.

V

I walk north toward my new home
past the abandoned house;
    the dry channels and ponds and fountains
    someone once made
        not quite believing
        they were in the desert.

I hear a whisper,
    not words
    something more delicate.

    I turn and go back.
    When I step onto the basalt path stones
    that lead to the house,

white pigeons

fly up from the eaves

hover

and

one by one

return.

I wrote those words a little over a year ago. A few months after I wrote the poem, I discovered a free no-money online slot machine site on the Internet. The first night I played from nine to ten thirty, the second night from nine to midnight. The third night I started in at nine and found myself hunched over the computer screen at four thirty in the morning. I logged off, crawled into bed, and knew I'd have to quit. I deleted the site from my bookmarks and, predictably, went through a week of feeling nuts. I didn't just tough it out. I called Candace and Sharon and told the truth to the Sisters.

Early in 2009, my life carried me into a friendship with a sister environmentalist in Washington State. She introduced me to a wildlife biologist who was looking for a writer to document a wilderness area she was fighting to save. I drove up to visit. I was surprised at how my body and brain seemed to relax in the bright, cool air, how my eyes felt soothed by gray light and the abundance of green. On the way back from my new friend's home, I stayed with longtime friends in Bend, Oregon. They joked, "You gotta move here. This is your town." It turned out to be no joke. A month later, I filled a U-Haul with my books and furniture, along with the help of my son and a friend.

I spent my last hours with Scheherazade's Sisters that night. They had understood my decision from the first night I had told them I was leaving. We are, after all, women of impulse. We are women who have followed the roller coaster of our lives. I promised the circle and myself that I would stay true to what we had all taught each other. When I went home that night, I walked out to the old Joshua Buddha and repeated my vow.

The next morning, I put my four cats in the back of the Vibe and drove north. I've been working on this book ever since. I found a compulsive gamblers' support group. It is not Scheherazade's Sisters, and yet the minute I sat in the circle of women and men, I felt at home. And I felt lucky. I do mean lucky.

There are gambling venues everywhere in Central Oregon. I haven't placed a casino bet since the $500 lesson in anger I write about in Chapter 10: "The Slip." But, a few weeks into living in my new home, I felt lonely. I returned to the free online slot machine site. Within two days the hook was set. I found myself crawling into bed at four in the morning. I crawled back out to delete the site from my bookmarks and called one of the other people in my GA group. It is to her credit that she answered the phone and listened.

The next day withdrawal flickered on the edges of my consciousness. This time I knew what was happening and didn't descend into the maelstrom. Instead, guided by the old twelve-step slogan, "More will be revealed," I logged on to the Internet. I was startled to find dozens of sites with the information on withdrawal I had so fruitlessly sought out. I understood that as casinos proliferated, the numbers of gambling addicts grew. As a bittersweet consequence, gambling addiction was finally being taken seriously by more than a few savvy addiction researchers and treatment professionals.

· Everything I found corroborated what I had experienced during withdrawal—and continue to experience whenever I catch myself falling back into compulsion and don't act on the urges. The information was both comforting—for a woman who always feels better when she understands what's under what she is feeling—and inarguable.

Gambling withdrawal can be marked by sweating, palpitations, depression, confusion, stomach troubles, headaches, increased physical tension, irritability, trouble concentrating, trouble listening, trouble remembering, agitation, inability to feel pleasure, and inability to look forward to future events. It is common for those in withdrawal to be driven by any of those symptoms to go back to gambling or to switch addictions. Every time I have quit gambling I've found myself obsessing about past loves and stocking the freezer with dulce de leche ice cream—the latter practice a far more satisfying drug.

The information on immediate withdrawal symptoms was illuminating and reassuring, but when I read about postacute withdrawal on a Victoria, Canada, Gamblers Anonymous site, missing pieces of a puzzle I'd never been able to solve fell into place. All of us who battle our compulsions and addictions talk about how easy it is to slip back into using—the recidivism rate for recovering gambling addicts is higher than that for any other addiction. We know, too, how hard it is to live clean. We can get blindsided by feelings that other people seem to take for granted. While I have come to understand the power of triggers, of euphoric recall, of a "disease that tells me it is not a disease," I have never fully accepted the depth and persistence of my mood swings—and the even-more-painful reality that I cannot seem to sustain ordinary happiness or remain interested in a loving relationship once it stabilizes.

Understanding postacute withdrawal has given me a new way to be with who I am. According to the GA Victoria website, postacute withdrawal can occur randomly at any time in recovery. It is hard to identify because it is not dependent on length of recovery. A ten-year-clean gambling addict can be plagued by it as much as the newly abstinent. While it can occur in connection with underlying psychological conditions like depression, bipolar, OCD, and other personality disorders, it is often misdiagnosed as one or more of those "illnesses." The website reads:

Often a deep emotional low occurs shortly after some pleasant experience like a good vacation, a promotion at work, a well deserved achievement or honor. The low is a baffling experience and is usually the point where the member goes back to the addiction, explodes uncontrollably or goes into a deep depression and is misdiagnosed.

When I read these words, I saw the template of decades of my life. I've used something—anything—to distract myself since I first discovered food and books when I was five or six. It's always been true that I need a good book to read to go to sleep, and when I don't have one or more of them I feel jittery. I've been an addict all my life. I've been in withdrawal all my life. Postacute withdrawal is an aftereffect of a true addict's cycles of using and withdrawing.

GA Victoria also discusses the phenomenon of a recovering gambler visiting a casino (not uncommon in areas in which casinos are also music and entertainment venues) and not gambling: "a few days or weeks later the same individual experiences an extreme mood swing—either a high or a low—and is again baffled. The effects of being in the gambling environment actually did trigger a delayed emotional reaction."

Finally, they reminded me that those of us who have used for years don't know what we feel. They point out that it's normal to have buildups of feelings—sadness, anger, frustration, anxiety, happiness, contentment, joy. Once the gambling addict is not using, those feelings can be overwhelming. "Reality is not a comfortable place for recovering addicts of any sort," the site emphasizes. And so, the recovering addict almost always reacts with a relapse of some kind, perhaps not by gambling, but by using any of the multitude of mind-altering substances and behaviors available to any of us.

It is a softly bright and cool September day in Bend as I finish writing this chapter. I feel an ease in my body, mind, and heart that I haven't felt in a long time. I've written the chapter I longed to read for so many years. It is the chapter that opens a new door to healing—for me and for many who might read this book. While what follows will be information about the hard work of that healing, it seems to me that providing some comfort to a woman facing the chaos and pain of withdrawal may be the most important payback to those who have helped me.

I've thought a lot about the last paragraphs of my long-ago message to Marilyn at Women Helping Women. I wish I had had the knowledge I needed to trust them seven years ago: *If any of you have just quit gambling and think you are going crazy, you're not. Go to meetings, call sober friends, call the national or local hotline. Reread my experience, strength, and hope, and know that you are going sane.*

WHAT IT TAKES

THE REALITY OF RECOVERING

The best gambling addiction treatment is to stop yourself. But if this does not help, other help is described here.

—Gambling Addiction Treatment, on Web4Health

No true addict ever recovers "from" an addiction. But any true addict may be able to recover "with" the addiction. For those of us who are true gambling addicts, the dream that someday we will be completely free of our compulsion is an illusion, as wishful and unreal as the hope we will someday be able to gamble normally.

The hardest truth I face on a daily basis is that my brain chemistry cannot be fixed. Unlike many, I cannot take antidepressants or mood stabilizers. I'm not even sure that I would take them if I could. The threads between my fragile nervous system and my fingers moving across the keyboard of my computer are tangled lifelines. I am my mother's girl.

She was a brilliant and gifted pianist who suffered for decades from near-annihilating bipolar psychosis. The psychiatrists of her time misdiagnosed her condition. She endured electroshock therapy, addictive barbiturates, and the ministrations of male doctors who believed that depressed women were hysterics who attempted suicide as bids for attention. Finally, sometime in the late '70s, her doctor gave her lithium. Her terrifying mood swings leveled out, but she called me one day and said, "I'm glad to not feel so blue, but, Mary Liz, when I play the piano, I can't feel anything inside. I can't feel the passion."

I was quiet. She and I were close by then. She knew I was listening. I was a writer and counselor who understood the trade-off she was making. "Oh well," she said, "that's the hell of it."

I've tried everything but medication to quit gambling: talk therapy, group therapy, practicing thought behavioral management, learning everything I could about the obsession, calling friends, white-knuckling it through a day or week or month of ferocious urges. I haven't used medications because my few experiences with antidepressants have been dreadful.

On my first attempt, my brain fast-forwarded into warp drive. I couldn't bear being in my skin. My mind was a hand grenade with the pin pulled. I managed somehow to meet with clients and my women's groups. To this day that seems a miracle, but I had learned as a little girl in the presence of my mother's transformations to move above the rattling terror and behave normally.

Two days into being on meds, I found myself at the mercy of suicidal thoughts—not in reaction to my discomfort, but appearing as simple declarative sentences from nowhere. *It would be so easy for a person to kill herself. I could drive eighty miles per hour into a tree. No one would know.*

By the fourth episode in three days of the calmly sinister thoughts, I'd had enough. I flushed the pills down the toilet, walked my neighborhood for three hours, and drank quarts of water. It seemed to take months for the sense of having swallowed a subtle poison to clear from my system. The psychiatrist who prescribed the meds knew about my low-level manic phases and had not warned me about the possibility of the pills triggering mania. All she had said was, "If you feel groggy, don't try to drive."

I tried medication once more, just before my mother's death in 1995. I took a half tablet of Zoloft, a selective serotonin reuptake inhibitor (SSRI). The mind launch was more immediate and far more intergalactic that time around. A psychiatric nurse friend happened to call me during the worst of what felt like being possessed by a chainsaw buzz. When I told her what I was experiencing, she told me I most likely had inherited a milder version of my mother's roller-coaster brain and that the antidepressant had triggered a temporary manic response.

She offered to come over and sit with me while I waited it out. I accepted. We walked on the long dirt road in front of my cabin. I swilled water. She told me stories of patients who had gone through the same reaction. "I'll never try that again," I said. "Is that a promise?" she said gently. "It's deeper than a promise," I said.

I have no judgments about psychoactive medications when they are prescribed appropriately, or about the people fortunate to be able to use them. I envy friends who can take antidepressants and experience no side effects. Both Barb and Candace swear by their meds and trust their counselors and prescribing psychiatrists. It makes sense for any woman facing gambling recovery to try whatever works. Medication may be one of the tools she can use. And it may not.

The evidence for the efficacy of pharmacotherapies for gambling addicts is somewhat in its infancy and sometimes contradictory, though both SSRIs and mood elevators seem to have some positive effects—especially in women with underlying mental or emotional disorders or other addictions (comorbidity). While this news is mildly good, the thoroughly discouraging news is that at the present time, there is no medication that specifically fixes dopamine imbalances—or the inherited inability to effectively utilize dopamine. Gambling binges can be a marker for onset of the high phase of bipolar disorder. And when it comes to depression, so many of the women I met in casinos talked about playing slots to cheer themselves up. There is also evidence that people with ADD find relief in the repetitive patterns of slot machines. It seems a paradox until one remembers that stimulants like caffeine and Ritalin also can reduce symptoms in ADD.

I suspect I have a graduate degree in comorbidity. Most of the women in Scheherazade's Sisters feel the same. All of us have gambled to medicate our feelings—to lower our highs, to jumpstart our highs, to lighten our bleak thoughts, to ease our sense of being overwhelmed by life. Of course, once we crossed the line into full-tilt addiction, we were also medicating our gambling withdrawal. We medicated the jones itself.

Barb and Candace both have battled depression for years. K-Siu believes that she may have lived with undiagnosed PTSD as the child of parents who had lost so much. Delfina took meds shortly after her suicide attempt and then began to face the role sexual abuse had played in her life.

I remember so many gambling trips that began with my obsessive-compulsive brainstorms—not bright ideas, but finding myself suddenly thinking I couldn't think. My miracle drug was my slot machine. The second I made the first bet, my brain stopped rattling. I could think through situations that had overwhelmed me. I could plan for the future. I could feel optimism about my life. I felt like myself again. Gambling was my medicine. I'd still use it if the side effects hadn't become intolerable.

It's important for anyone evaluating the choice to take a medication to work with a trained mental health professional, preferably a gambling treatment psychologist, psychiatrist, counselor, social worker, or nurse. Mental and physical health professionals not trained in the specifics of gambling addiction often are not able to fully understand the complexity of the compulsion.

My history with talk therapy for my gambling addiction may be atypical. I worked with three different caring, principled, and gifted talk therapists, two in private counseling, one as a group facilitator. We probed into my childhood, my history of other addictions and compulsions. We discussed my impulsiveness and my mood swings. I worked the first four of the twelve steps with the group therapist. I experienced each of these competent professionals as caring. I felt free to open up about everything.

And I gambled. Sometimes intermittently. Sometimes rarely. I never lied to the therapists. I told them that I knew I had to quit—and I didn't want to. We tried behavior modification, identifying activities that could replace gambling (writing, hiking, and environmental activism were all I could think of), thought monitoring, keeping a gambling journal, recording dollar losses, paying attention to my feelings waking up after a gambling binge, my lies, and my excuses.

I tried everything. And I gambled.

I credit my therapists with much. I didn't sink into despair. I didn't drink or drug or eat myself into oblivion. I wrote. I drew slowly away from an unfortunate and compelling love affair. I didn't move to Laughlin, take a job as a buffet hostess, and gamble out the rest of my life. I didn't kill myself, either intentionally or by unconsciously behaving in such a way that would result in a fatal injury or terminal illness.

We talk often in Scheherazade's Sisters about how therapy or treatment helped us stay alive long enough to come to the moments that stopped us cold. Our therapists worked with a broad range of counseling and behavioral techniques: CBT (cognitive-behavioral therapy); systematic desensitization (to reduce the anxiety that for so many gamblers precipitates a binge); behavior modification; traditional psychotherapy (the examination of childhood factors in establishment of emotional disorders and addictions); EMDR (eye movement desensitization and reprocessing); exploration of the effects of PTSD; Jungian analysis; and more.

It seems that one of the most effective clinical interventions for the gambling addict is CBT, in part because it gives addicts practical tools to deal with their gambling urges and impulses.

CBT teaches clients to note thoughts and emotions that occur in response to an environmental cue and that precede their behavioral response to the stimulus. CBT involves their learning to challenge the validity of their responses, then choosing to change their addictive behaviors, perhaps replacing the addictive behavior with a different pleasurable activity, perhaps imagining dire consequences specific to the behavior, perhaps choosing to imagine that they avoid the behavior and then consciously avoiding the behavior.

I've practiced my own version of mind training for decades, long before I learned about it. I remember the first moment I realized that my panic had nothing to do with reality, and the immediate awareness that nothing external was going to permanently remove my fear. I was twenty-three, married, and had just given birth to my third child. My husband worked a day job. I was at home with the kids. I ran out of milk and decided to go to the store. I'd put the baby in the stroller and had my toddler daughter's hand in mine, her other hand in her brother's hand.

We lived in a little lakeside shack a few blocks from a neighborhood grocery. I moved our caravan out the door and onto the street and looked down the gentle slope toward the store. Suddenly, the ground trembled under my feet. The houses on either side of the street seemed to be leaning in on me. My hands went numb. I couldn't draw a deep breath. I was sure I was having a brain aneurysm.

I began to turn the stroller around so I could flee back into the house. And then I thought of my mother, her bleak silences, her lacerating outbursts, her transformations from mother into black hole. I kept my feet planted on the asphalt. My son said, "Did you forget something?" I didn't trust myself to speak, certainly not to say, "Oh yes I did. I forgot that I carry a promise in me that the three of you will never go through what I did." Instead, I pulled a deep breath into my body past what felt like a concrete block. "I was just thinking that we have to get ice cream, too." My son laughed. I took a step forward, then another, then another.

I still practice walking through difficulties. After that moment, it became impossible for me to not take action when I don't want to and know I must. Walking through has nothing to do with courage. I know that if I give in to the fear that has arisen, I will make it stronger. Walking through has carried me on a Class VI rapid on the Colorado River, up a slick-rock slope in monsoon lightning, away from believing I was responsible for every human being I met, toward this life in which I know I have no idea what comes next. More than anything, walking through brings me to every word I pour onto the page. But walking through solo could not walk me away from a slot machine when I was determined to play.

No matter what form of therapy a woman compulsive gambler chooses, it's important that she try to find a therapist who has been educated and trained to work with gamblers. Because recognition of gambling addiction is in its infancy, it can be difficult, if not impossible, to find a gambling-savvy therapist. But there are Internet resources that can help. The National Council on Problem Gambling (NCPG) provides resources not just for the gambling addict seeking recovery, but for concerned family and friends and mental health professionals as well. NCPG is an up-to-date and compassionate ally in the difficult work of decoding the maze of our gambling lives and finding the pathway out through recovery.

NCPG suggests criteria for choosing a therapist for gambling addiction. According to their website:

[A] Certified Gambling Counselor is defined as an individual who has completed a specific course of study in problem gambling treatment and has been certified by either:

- A national credentialing organization (National Gambling Counselor Certification Board–NCGC; American Gambling Counselor Certification Board–CCGC; or American Academy of Health Care Providers in the Addictive Disorders–CAS); or
- A state certification organization that requires a minimum of 30 hours of problem gambling specific training and a period of direct (supervisor personal contact) supervision related to treating addicted gamblers.

NCPG's website has a list of certified counselors and treatment centers throughout the United States.

Only some of us in Scheherazade's Sisters have been able to afford, or have had the medical insurance to pay for, a residential treatment center. To compound the difficulty, there are few centers available. The NCPG describes residential treatment programs as

organized and staffed to provide both general and specialized non-hospital-based interdisciplinary services 24 hours a day, 7 days a week. Residential treatment services are organized to provide environments in which the persons reside and receive services from *personnel who are trained in the delivery of services for persons with behavioral health disorders or related problems. Residential treatment may be provided in freestanding, non-hospital-based facilities or in units of larger entities, such as a wing of a hospital. Residential treatment programs may include domestic violence treatment homes, non-hospital addiction treatment centers, intermediate care facilities, psychiatric treatment centers, or other non-medical settings.*

Inpatient treatment programs are set in hospitals. They provide coordinated and integrated services in hospital settings. Inpatient treatment is provided 24 hours, 7 days a week. Inpatient treatment programs include a comprehensive, bio-psychosocial-spiritual approach to service delivery with a key component being close coordination of services with other service providers and organizations who may be involved in service provision for the persons served. There are daily therapeutic activities in which the persons served participate. The goal of inpatient treatment is to provide a protective environment that includes medical stabilization, support, treatment for psychiatric or addictive disorders, and supervision. Such programs operate in designated space that allows for an appropriate medical treatment environment.

The National Council on Problem Gambling maintains a list of gambling treatment centers (and counselors) that meet their minimum standards for qualifications. In addition, the NCPG website suggests questions a gambling addict considering treatment might ask:

If you or someone you care for needs treatment for a gambling problem, it is important to know that no single treatment approach is appropriate for all individuals. Finding the right treatment program involves careful consideration of such things as the setting, length of care, philosophical approach and your or your loved one's needs. We encourage you to thoroughly investigate your options.

Here are 12 questions to consider asking when selecting a gambling treatment program:

1. Are their counselors and staff experienced in treating problem gamblers? (How many problem gamblers are currently in their program; how many problem gamblers have they treated in the past year; what percentage of the patients are problem gamblers)?

2. How many hours per day are dedicated to gambling specific treatment or education? What are the groups or educational topics that address the specific needs of problem gamblers and their families?

3. Does the program accept your insurance? If not, will they work with you on a payment plan or find other means of support for you?

4. Does the program encompass the full range of assessment and treatment needs of the individual/family (medical: including universal precautions for infectious diseases; psychological: including co-occurring substance abuse and mental health problems; financial: money management, budgeting and restitution; social; vocational; legal; spiritual; etc.)?

5. Does the treatment program also address sexual orientation and physical disabilities as well as provide age, gender and culturally appropriate services?

6. Is long-term continuing care support and/or guidance encouraged, provided and maintained?

7. Is there ongoing assessment of an individual's treatment plan to ensure it meets changing needs?

8. Does the program employ strategies to engage and keep individuals in treatment, increasing the likelihood of success?

9. Does the program offer counseling (individual and group) and other behavioral therapies to enhance the individual's ability to function in the family/community?

10. Does the program offer medication as part of the treatment regimen, if appropriate?

11. Is there ongoing monitoring of possible relapse?

12. Are services or referrals offered to family members to ensure they understand problem gambling, its impact on the family and the recovery process?

(Adapted from "A Quick Guide to Finding Effective Drug and Alcohol Treatment, Center for Substance Abuse Treatment," 2002)

I thought about finding a treatment center when the raw OCD took my brain hostage in the 2008 Mojave winter. I called Larayne, my trusted adviser, and the first thing she asked me was if I was suicidal. "No," I said, "but I keep thinking that I have two choices: I go through this without using or I kill myself. The latter is not an option. I'm too chicken—and I want to see the desert wildflowers this spring."

She laughed. She knew my fears of dementia. "You can rest easy on your dementia diagnosis," she said. "I just read an article that said that people with dementia are incapable of irony or sarcasm."

"At least I'm spared that," I said. "It's the 3:00 AM awakenings that make me want to run to someplace safe, someplace where I'd know I wasn't alone."

"I can just see you in treatment," she said. "(A) you know everything the staff knows; (B) they'd want to prescribe meds; and (C) you'd be locked up."

My fantasized safety net shimmered and was gone. "Besides," I said, "they'd figure I was delusional, imagining I could afford them. I don't have any money, and my only insurance is Medicare."

"Okay," Larayne told me, "I have an idea. Treatment centers almost all use the twelve-step principles. What if you found all the open Alcoholics and Narcotics Anonymouses you could find in the area and went to as many as you could. You could identify as an addict, or you could keep your mouth shut and just listen. You've got your Scheherazade's circle, and there are GA meetings down in the Valley. I know how much you love the circle, but maybe it's time to branch out.

"You work at home, so you can make your own hours. Keep walking, keep talking to friends, keep doing nothing when you can stand to do nothing. I truly believe the nothing is what contains the grace, and maybe some knowledge."

I knew she was right. "So," I said, "I get myself to a lot of meetings, sit on my hands, and don't use. . . . "

"And call me at least once a day," she cut in. "Five times a day, once an hour, whatever it takes."

I put myself into in-house treatment for forty-five days. I marked my calendars with green Xs. As each day passed, I drew a red heart over the Xs. It felt corny and irritatingly touchy-feely, but I needed a visible reminder that time was passing and I was still somewhat coherent.

I was running out of money. I'd found no work the whole year in the Morongo Basin despite a relentless search. I offered a writing circle, but no one had any extra money for frills. The area was a microcosm for high gas prices in a sinking American economy. My steady-state fear about paying rent, buying food, and not losing my car added a barbed wire edge to the underlying OCD. I reminded myself I was not alone in that worry. It was easy to remember. Every day I went to meetings and heard other people talk about lost jobs, lost houses, lost trucks and cars.

I had just enough money to get to the end of my in-home treatment. I decided that a woman in a treatment program wouldn't be looking for work, so I stopped my futile hunt. I'd concentrate on working on the women and gambling book, go to twelve-step meetings and Scheherazade's Sisters, call friends, and sit on my hands the rest of the time.

As soon as I moved my thoughts away from worrying about money, all the other fears kicked in—brain tumor, stroke, never being able to read again, diabetes-induced brain rot, deadly skin-eating disease, everything but coming down with Ebola virus. There were many moments when all I could manage was to not log on and find an online slot game or the email address of a former lover. Instead I sat in my old rocking chair, looked out on the sweet winter desert, and said "Thank you" to Who-Knows-What that I wasn't raising kids or grandkids, sleeping in my car, or having to drag myself into a job I hated.

December 31 I drew the last red heart on my calendar. I didn't feel "happy, joyous, and free," as recovering alcoholics often speak of feeling or expecting to feel. I didn't even feel content. All I could feel was, "I made it through that—for now." The next day I woke terrified about money. I wrote friends, students, and readers and offered them a weekly essay subscription for whatever they wanted to pay. Their generosity began to trickle, then flood in. I was covered for the next few months.

Slowly, sometimes imperceptibly, the worse aspects of the OCD began to fade. A work opportunity arrived unexpectedly. It took me to Washington State for a month in April. On the drive back, I realized that I couldn't go through another Mojave summer—not only the heat and glare, but the economic drought that was devastating jobs throughout California. With the new clarity of not using, I understood that without using I needed to make a life that held some daily comfort. That's what precipitated the move to Bend. There is no Scheherazade's Sisters here, but there are warm and welcoming Gamblers Anonymous meetings.

I don't know if in-house treatment could work for anyone else. I had the gifts of Scheherazade's Sisters, open twelve-step meetings, a wise adviser who continually educated herself about recovery tactics and options, a schedule free from external pressure, no responsibility for anyone other than myself, a long history of knowledge about growth and my resistance to it, a book to write about precisely what I was going through, friends who battle addiction on a daily basis, the Mojave desert as my chapel, and a vague sense that there just might be something bigger than myself—that didn't want to punish me.

There is ample evidence in gambling recovery literature that some people stop on their own—the money runs out; a partner's and/or family's patience is gone; gamblers become disgusted with their own behavior; they become frightened at their inability to control their gambling; debts pile up, and their creditors are not credit card companies, but dangerous people. Those who stop on their own often use many of the same techniques they might have learned in therapy or support groups, or turn to religion and/or spiritual practices for strength.

Some gambling addicts who do not seek therapy might say that they didn't figure their gambling problem was serious enough for professional help; they didn't know help was available; they couldn't afford it; they were too ashamed of their lack of self-control to talk about it with others. Since there is no way to determine how many compulsive gamblers have quit on their own, there is no way to know how many have stayed clean and how many have returned to gambling.

I do know that I can't stay away from my next first bet alone. I credit the sisterhood and the compassion and honesty I found in Scheherazade's Sisters for much of what success I have had in my recovery. But without my experiences in Gamblers Anonymous, I would eventually forget what I learned in that circle.

Gamblers Anonymous is a miracle. By all laws of good corporate business practices, it should not exist. There are no leaders. There is no real hierarchy. Nobody pays to belong. Nobody makes a penny off the members. Despite the Twelve Traditions, there are no real rules. There are only suggestions.

Though spiritual conditions are talked about, there is no overarching universal god, no priests, no commandments, no penance, no heaven or hell. Believing in something greater than oneself is not a condition of membership. The only criteria for entrance into GA's circles of connection is the desire to stop gambling.

GA is not perfect. Tyrants arise. Members ignore the conventions of not giving advice, not gossiping, not preaching. Meetings fade away. GA members go back out and gamble. Some return, some do not. GA, after all, is nothing but a worldwide gathering of human beings.

Before I move on to write about my time in this program, I want to reassure any of the people with whom I have sat (and sit) in GA meetings that their anonymity is sealed in my heart. My own anonymity is not easy to give up, but since I am anything but a perfect GA practitioner who might fall from grace someday, I am not afraid that any woman reading this book will judge GA by my ever-present potential fallibility.

Gamblers Anonymous sprang up in 1957. Two men came together to deal with their mutual gambling addictions. According to GA's history, " . . . [T]hey used for a guide certain spiritual principles which had been utilized by thousands of people who were recovering from other compulsive addictions. The word spiritual can be said to describe those characteristics of the human mind that represent the highest and finest qualities such as kindness, generosity, honesty and humility. Also, in order to maintain their own abstinence they felt that it was vitally important that they carry the message of hope to other compulsive gamblers."

And they might as well have been genius brain researchers. The basic mechanisms of GA, as I use them, are (1) Don't make the first bet and (2) Keep coming back. The basic neurochemical mechanism of gambling addiction is that once the first bet is made, the brain of the gambling addict is swamped by a flash flood of dopamine and other neurotransmitters. The flash flood carries the compulsive gambler forward to the next bet, the hundredth bet, the thousandth bet.

If the first bet is not made, there is no flood. But for the true addict, there is then the hard work of living with a brain that hungers for the fix. Only in Scheherazade's Sisters and GA have I found others who understand exactly how harrowing living clean can be—and who hold out hope that there is life beyond withdrawal. If Scheherazade's Sisters existed in my new home, I would take myself to the circle every week.

There is a third component of GA that I have found invaluable—the twelve steps. The twelve steps are a progression of mental and behavioral (and for many, spiritual) exercises that some GA members use as a means of rigorous self-examination and behavior change—and some use as links to a spiritual connection. I've worked the steps again and again. Each time, they bring me closer to living with some grace with the limitations that any addict does not want to embrace—and must.

While I've met recovering people in GA who describe their lives as happy, I've met more who are grateful to be free from acting on their urges, but who talk openly about their lives being anything but blissful. I know few recovering gamblers who think of their newfound lives in the terms "happy, joyous, and free," like some recovering alcoholics do—we have gratitude for what we are learning, for what we have regained, and for what we give each other, but we seem to have a less-ebullient view of life after gambling.

Alcohol and gambling are very different drugs. I suspect that many gambling addicts, especially those of us who hid in our slot machines, are also different from their alcoholic kin. In my experience, recovering alcoholics tend to be more outgoing, more gregarious, and less driven by rules. I've found that we gambling addicts can be more thin-skinned, in more need of control in our lives, and significantly more anxious.

I am thin-skinned, controlling—whether I'm using or not—and *always* anxious. To hear others speak of feeling happy, joyous, and free has always made me feel less than. I should have tried harder. I should have been more grateful. I should have lost myself in caring for others. I was a privileged American brat.

So it is always more comforting for me to listen to others talk about how difficult gambling addiction recovery can be. If I've had a rough day, I can easily feel connection. It's common in twelve-step programs for beginners to be encouraged to hang with members who "have what you want." I want, more than anything, to live in the fierce light of reality, so it is toward the realists that I move.

When I think back on my years of halfhearted efforts to stop gambling, I now understand that the time I spent in individual and group therapy helped me slowly learn. By the time I made serious commitments to Scheherazade's Sisters and GA, I had taken apart a rotting foundation. I suspect I was ready to build something new. I needed therapy, and I need my groups.

I am not alone in that. Dr. Nancy Petry, a widely respected professor of psychiatry at the University of Connecticut, writes in her 2005 *Pathological Gambling: Etiology, Comorbidity and Treatment* that " . . . [S]ome gamblers receive assistance from both professional and self-help modalities. Some data suggest that the effectiveness of GA can be enhanced by concurrent participation in professional treatment programs." Dr. Robert Hunter, founder and director of International Problem Gambling Centers, goes a step further. He tells someone who wants to be his client that participating in Gamblers Anonymous is mandatory; it is not just an option. He feels that the numbers tell the story, and the numbers indicate that a combination of therapy and GA can benefit most compulsive gamblers. "If somebody wants to see me," he says, "and won't go to GA, I refuse them as a client. I don't do this to be politically correct, or curry favor with GA. I do this because it's the most ethical thing I can offer my clients."

Many recovering gamblers, whether GA members or not, believe that their higher power—God, Goddess, the Divine, the Universe, Grandfather and Grandmother, Wakan Tanka, healing energy, Buddha, Allah, something unnamed, nonhuman, and greater—is the critical element in their recovery. They speak of being carried, guided, and loved to wellness.

When I first dabbled in twelve-step meetings, I had a neighbor who swore that my mean old tabby cat, Big Guy, had brought him to enlightenment. My friend was sunk in depression over a relationship—not an uncommon condition for addicts! He'd finally gotten on his knees to pray to a god he didn't believe in. Big Guy wandered in through the open door. "Please help me," my friend whimpered. At that instant, Big Guy took a swipe at my friend's face and laid open his cheek. My friend told us that all he could do was break into laughter. "That was it," he said. "I was yanked off my pity pot, and I was *saved!*"

I have no fixed notion of my higher power. I much prefer the notion of a greater power, of a vastness that is all-encompassing, an energy that is not "above" me but around me. Earth, air, water, light, and darkness. I made it through the harsh Mojave winter of deep withdrawal, disassociation, and OCD using every tool I had—walking in the quiet twilight desert out to the dead Joshua tree that seemed, at twilight, to be a seated Buddha; reaching out to loving friends; sitting tight with all of me when all of me wanted to run away; talking with some greater something that I suspected was no more than a human-created symbol of the infinite.

A banner of a Tibetan Buddhist deity, Mahakala, hangs on my wall. I believe that Mahakala, be "he" god or principle of life, eats the obstacles to my joy. By "joy" I don't mean intoxication or even happiness. By joy I mean full immersion in this life I am privileged to live, life with all the fear and peacefulness, irritability and contentment, desire and disappointment, sweetness and resignation I feel—usually all of them in any single day.

Most of the time the Mahakala banner is covered with a sequined red, black, and yellow gauze. I have learned that in Tibet, Mahakala's abilities are so respected and feared that many of his shrines contain nothing but a piece of black cloth. To gaze on him is to risk the unbearable. I have also been taught that places and objects of power can be misused. In addition, I've witnessed spiritual greed in others and myself—the pilgrimage of the privileged from one guru to another, from one self-awareness workshop to the next, always asking, "Please help me," never coming up to the immovable wall that turns us inward to the emptiness we all contain. So I turn to Mahakala rarely.

As the OCD worsened, I decided to unveil Mahakala. Each morning I stood before him and said, "I offer you everything that is in the way of my joy." Each time I knew that my words were a one-way road away from using. Each time I felt no comfort, only surrender. When the forty-five days of in-home treatment were over, I thanked the satin image of a huge face with a gaping maw. I draped the sparkling gauze over it. I wondered when next I would uncover him.

No matter what therapeutic interventions provide, no matter the excellence of a treatment center, no matter the efficacy of a medicine, no matter how committed a recovering gambler is to a twelve-step program, no matter what higher power an addict finds or doesn't find, the moment continues to come when the gambling addict either stops or goes forward into financial, mental, familial, and societal ruin. I've come to believe that much of my life as an addict is, and will be, occupied with "not doing," with being willing to go into whatever feelings arise when I don't "do," with accepting that my healing is slow and will be incomplete—and in moving deep as I can into each moment of unaltered reality as it arises before me.

As I walk through this knowledge, I carry with me the words of a GA old-timer. She tells us often that when people ask her how GA works, she always says, "It works great."

And it doesn't cost a fortune—or a penny.

THE SLIP
WHY SHE GOES BACK OUT

You've got three kinds of recovering gambling addicts:
those who've slipped,
those who could slip,
those who could slip again.

—Janelle, five years clean

A year into my last stretch of not gambling I took on an out-of-town writing job in Washington State. I'd be working with a wildlife biologist who knew a wilderness area better than the wildlife did. I knew I'd have to hike in the wilderness area myself because I write from place, and to occupy place I have to have my feet solid on the ground and my nose to the wind.

I love road trips. I find leaving home terrifying. The two facts do not override each other. I drove away from my cabin both jittery and grateful that my research adviser in the north was becoming a friend. I knew I could rely on her for check-ins as I made the long trip.

The drive took almost three days. My friend seemed to disappear after I'd been on the road for three hours. I couldn't reach her by phone. When I stopped for lunch, I emailed, "Hey, where are you?" I didn't hear from her that day. I felt a little irritated, but the sky above the Sierras was turquoise and the air so warm I drove with my windows down, and I had time to stop at a huge obsidian flow south of Mono Lake. I grabbed a huge turkey sandwich at Erick Schat's in Bishop, felt the tryptophan flood my brain, and was nothing but optimistic.

I stayed with a friend in Reno. We went out for Thai food. She took a shortcut, smack through glittering downtown Reno. I grabbed the dashboard. Naomi looked at me. "I am *so* sorry. I completely forgot," she said, "are you okay?"

I laughed. "I'm doing great for somebody who didn't just jump out of a car going forty miles an hour."

We made it to the Thai restaurant. Naomi asked all the right questions. I was relieved to find that I had the right answers. When we were done eating, we drove back home the long way.

The next day the March weather went bipolar. Sleet glazed my windshield. I knew there were winding roads ahead and a high mountain pass. I checked into a small-town motel and Googled the weather forecast. The pass was open, but likely to close by dark. I checked my email. No message from my friend. No phone call. I wanted to smack her. I looked out the motel window. A scarlet sign glittered in the distance. Casino.

It took one second of irritation with my friend and six big, glowing letters a few blocks away for me to pull on my coat, grab my purse, and head down the stairs. Five minutes later I walked into the casino, pulled 100 bucks (I was practicing moderation) out of the ATM, converted it to fives, and headed for the banks of slot machines.

The casino was a big, smoky, warehouse-style joint. The huge room where the slots were lined up was about two-thirds empty space, with about a tenth of the machines occupied. I was glad. I'd managed to pump my irritation up into righteous rage. I didn't want to make talk with anybody. I was there for the buzz and the numb. I knew I was playing "against my friend." It's addict slang for being furious with someone or something and gambling for vengeance.

The slot machines were not my allies. Two and a half hours and 500 bucks later, I slunk up to the ATM machine and thought, *I'm bored.*

I drove back to the motel, walked to a little taqueria, bought dinner, and settled into my room. The tacos were the real deal, homemade, the chicken and cilantro fresh, the tortillas thick and soft. I wolfed down the first one, then slowed down. The cilantro's green scent cut through my crankiness. I looked at myself in the motel mirror. My addict self grinned back. She shrugged her shoulders. "Oh well, sometimes the magic works, and sometimes it doesn't."

As my blood sugar adjusted I realized I needed more company than my addict's bemused self. I called my two best friends and my trusted adviser. They listened. They each said the same thing: "Hey, you're an addict. Do you want to go back and win back what you lost?" When I answered, one of them said, "Okay, take the book you brought for the trip out of your backpack, climb in bed, and read till you fall asleep." Larayne said, "Now you know a few more of your triggers. You feel abandoned, you get pissed off, and you want vengeance."

"Well, that's a plus," I said. "It might have taken four shrink sessions at $125 a pop minimum, and I still might not have gotten it."

Larayne laughed. "Nice," she said, "you're still holding dementia at bay. But I'm not going to let you get away with minimizing going out. That'd make it too easy for you to do it again. It wasn't a slip. It was a series of reactions and choices."

"Thanks for the pep talk," I said. "Seriously, thanks."

"One more thing," she said, "when you get to Bellingham, find a bunch of open meetings and get your butt to one tomorrow."

I got lucky with my relapse. Five hundred bucks is about half my monthly living expenses, but that five hundred didn't metastasize into a thousand. I woke the next morning, gulped down two cups of wan motel coffee, packed, and took myself back on the road before I could decide to return to the casino determined to win back what I'd lost. I stopped for breakfast in a mom 'n' pop diner a half hour north of the casino. I was almost joyful to be hungry, to look around the little joint and not feel pissed off at everybody I saw—most "mornings after" in my gambling life I'd had no appetite and despised humanity. I wrote in my journal as I waited for my waffle and eggs. "*Escaped this time. Good enough for now.*"

I drove up to my writing partner's house. I rang the bell. It took a long time for someone to answer. Ella opened the door. Her face was pale, her eyes red, her hair a tangle of snarls. "Come in," she said, "your room's upstairs on the right. I've got to go back to bed. I had food poisoning."

I unpacked. I realized I was anxious and hungry. Ella lived in a working-class neighborhood a few blocks from downtown. I checked on her, found her asleep, and went out for a walk. As my body and brain relaxed, I knew I needed to tell her what had happened. All of it. There was something about her raw honesty when she greeted me at the door that deserved mine in return. And, I knew I needed to eat. There's an old saying in twelve-step meetings: "Watch out for HALT: Hungry, Angry, Lonely, Tired. If you're feeling any of them, halt what you're doing and take care of yourself."

Ella emerged from her room that evening. I sat in the kitchen finishing off an order of chicken enchiladas from a nearby restaurant. "That actually looks good," she said. "I'm amazed. I figured I'd never eat again."

"There's more on the counter," I said. "Help yourself." She laughed. "So, what a welcome to the North Country!" She put one enchilada on a plate, eyed it warily, made peppermint tea, and sat down with me.

"I am so sorry," she said. "I went from perfectly normal to doubled-up in front of the toilet in a second. All I could do for three days was haul myself to the bathroom, drink water, and collapse back in bed. I figured that what with you being another solo woman, you'd be okay—and you'd understand."

It takes me a minute, but I finally say, "I'm fine. But I had a little glitch on the way up."

She grinned. "Let me guess. I've read some of your work. The big red sign on the Quonset hut at Spirit Lake sucked you right in."

"It did."

Ella waved at the cupboard behind her. "If you look in there, sister, you'll find my gin. We all gotta have a little something. I quit. I drink. I quit. I drink. At the moment, I'm not drinking."

"There's more," I said. "I got really pissed off when I didn't hear from you."

"I don't blame you," she said.

We put our dishes in the sink, moved into her cozy living room, and talked for the next few hours about the battles we'd fought (and still fight) with our compulsions. She handed me a list of AA and NA meetings and said there was at least one GA meeting in the area. By the time we both went off to bed, we knew each other in the way that addicts can. I thought, as I do so often, that honesty and fallibility were gifts. We hadn't had time or inclination for polite chitchat. My writing partner and hostess was a new friend.

Ella took me into the wilderness area every few days. She named the beauty I marveled at—the giant ferns and ancient red cedar, the red-tailed hawk and the delicate lizard. I had hours of time alone in my room to write—and to think back on my history of relapses. From the moment I'd first set foot in the gambling therapy group at least a decade earlier, I had never stayed clean longer than a year. It was typical for me to get a month, two months, *maybe* six months of not gambling under my belt and then, in a millisecond, decide to go to the casino. I knew the statistics. I knew that about two-thirds of recovering gamblers coming out of treatment relapsed in the first three months. I knew that the recidivism rate for recovering gamblers was higher than that for any other addiction. I knew that proximity of a casino to the recovering gambler exponentially increased the possibility that she would relapse.

There was still something unexamined about my recent relapse. I didn't discover it until I talked to Helen a few days later. She told me that Barb had not shown up for one meeting, then a second. Because we have an agreement in Scheherazade's Sisters not to "smother-love" each other, Candace waited till the third week to call. Barb didn't answer, return the call, text, or email back. When Candace told the group Barb seemed to have disappeared, they all suspected what was happening.

Barb showed up for the next meeting. "She looked like a whipped pup," Helen told me. "She said she knew what had happened. She'd called one of her credit card companies to try to set up smaller payments. The representative told her that wouldn't be possible because her income was so small. Then she went to her bank to see if she could get a loan to help out with the payments. They told her that with her "unfortunate" history, she couldn't get a loan—even with her golden credit record with them. You know she's paid back almost all the money she took from the church. That didn't count for anything with her bank.

"So she said she just thought, *F–it, I'm sick of being good*; took the 50 bucks she had in her purse; and went to the casino. She lost a bundle. But she said she drove home and all she could think was, *So, I still owe all that money to the credit cards, and now I've got 56 bucks in my savings and 300 till the end of the month—and I feel like shit. And, I know it's going to take forever for my brain to get back to normal.*"

"Well," I said, "Barb's not the only one. I got pissed off at somebody and looked out my motel window and saw a casino sign, and that was it."

Helen snapped back. "What the hell were you doing in a motel near a casino?"

I was so surprised by her anger that I couldn't speak. "Are you there?" she asked.

"I am."

"Do you hate me for being such a nag?" Helen replied. "I'm sorry, honey, it just seemed to me that you were fooling yourself."

"I'm not mad at you," I said. "It never occurred to me to think about why, of all the towns on the way to Bellingham, I decided to stay in the one with a casino. I think I'd planned the whole thing from the minute I started getting mad at my friend. I know I did."

"Well good," Helen said firmly. "What I've gone through has *got* to help somebody. I'm glad it's you."

I thanked her and said, "See you in a month."

I hung up and thought about my words to Larayne: "Shit, it might have taken four shrink sessions at $125 a pop minimum, and I still might not have gotten it." I'm a seat-of-the-pants learner—and a hard case—when it comes to knowing what I have to know to change my behavior. I was grateful that it had taken only 500 bucks to shed light on part of what had driven me for the last eight to nine years of my gambling history. I was even more grateful that I now knew what to look out for.

Some people in twelve-step recovery refer to relapse as a "slip." I don't. Even before I did the research for this book, I had always had hunches that when I gave in to the urge to use—be it contacting an unavailable former lover when I'd promised myself I wouldn't; grabbing a sixth chocolate chip cookie; pouring myself a third gin and soda when I knew I had to get up at 6:00 AM; suddenly finding myself pulling into the casino ninety minutes from my cabin with 60 bucks in my wallet, 40 in my savings, 100 in checking, and three credit cards I had yet to max out—I'd made not one choice, but a series of choices.

True gambling addicts, whether they have a genetic predisposition or not, are playing against a canny dealer with a stacked deck. And whether The Dealer is the casinos or my own longings for relief, vengeance, or constant excitement, there is no way for me to win.

I believe that when it comes to a relapse in a true addict, post-acute withdrawal rules. I think of the words on the GA Victoria website: "Reality is not a comfortable place for recovering addicts of any sort" and "This is the phenomenon that happens when a 20 year veteran of a 12-step program goes back to his/her addiction and leaves everyone scratching their heads in disbelief."

Robert R. Perkinson's powerful self-help guide, *The Gambling Addiction Patient Workbook,* lists thirty-seven warning signs that point to relapse. All of them fit with the discomfort and anhedonia that a recovering gambler in postacute withdrawal can experience. As I read the list, I found myself keeping count: apprehension about well-being—check; denial—check; compulsive attempts to impose abstinence on others—I'd tried to "cure" every one of my friends in Flagstaff who was still using; defensiveness—check; compulsive behavior—ha!; loneliness—90 percent of the time; plans beginning to fail— welcome to the collapse of the publishing world as I had known it; irritations with friends—check and check and check.

Barb and I made it back into not gambling. Many women don't. In the year I sat with the Scheherazade's Sisters, I listened to a dozen or so women who hung out with us for a week, weeks, even months, and then disappeared without a message to any of us. Each of us understood. We all knew how insidious our addictions were.

We've each spoken of the dozens or hundreds of times we vowed to stop and didn't. For some those failures of willpower were agonizing. Delfina has said more than once that it was her shame over being unable to quit that drove her to the suicide attempt that saved her life.

I was less guilt-ridden by my relapses, but I am at so many levels a hippie seminarcissist. In part because of my seminarcissism, I have no partner. My sons and daughter are grown and independent. I refuse to be responsible for anyone other than myself, so I never let anyone down. And, I don't gauge my worth or another person's by wealth—in fact, my judgments fall not on the poor, but the rich. Money had never seemed real to me, until my acute terror during that Mojave winter. Only recently have I begun to manage what money I have responsibly.

Being financially prudent makes me feel trapped. But, I'm sixty-nine now with no retirement except for Social Security. The time I spent homeless in my twenties convinced me that there is nothing charming about bag ladies—or outlaw life on the streets. So, it's time to grow up.

The other Sisters and I talk often about our amazement that we aren't sitting side-by-side in front of a row of slot machines instead of in a shabby room in an adult center. We know what it has taken and takes to show up once a week with another seven days of not using. We talk, usually hesitantly, about grace. Some of us believe in it, some don't. What we all believe in is the power of the tools we've learned and taught to each other that *can* work.

Here are a few steps a recovering addict can take to stay away from a relapse. They fall in line with a wonderful story that often makes the rounds of twelve-step meetings: Gal walks down a street, falls in a hole. Next time, she walks toward same hole, tells herself it isn't there, and falls in. Next walk down the street, she takes the other side of the street. Finally, she chooses another street.

GA teaches that a gambling addict cannot go near or in a casino with impunity. I've heard a dozen times that someone who slipped decided they'd just go into the casino to use the restroom, get a cup of coffee, see if it still held allure. The hole was right in front of them, and they marched straight toward it.

It is in "going down a different street" that we might find the safest route. There are at least a dozen websites now available to the recovering gambler who senses a relapse coming on. Their tips for avoiding relapse can be condensed into four simple steps. I keep a separate journal for my personal relapse notes. I've listed these steps in my notebook and written my responses to them. Parts of my responses are in italics here:

1. Prevention—when you are in strong recovery, learn your triggers and warning signs . . .

My most powerful triggers are boredom, anger, and euphoric recall. My strongest warning signs are restlessness, feeling abandoned by friends, resentment, and apprehension about my well-being.

. . . and stay away from casinos and casino advertisements. Many recovering gambling addicts ban themselves from their favorite casinos. The casinos participate in the ban.

7/9/09: I hear people talk about how easy it is to gamble here in Bend. Apparently, the state has lottery slot machines in bars and liquor stores. A friend tells me there is a sign with crossed fingers on it. He says he takes the sign to mean "Stay away."

As I drive around on my errands, I get glimpses of the signs and consciously look away.

2. The urge hits—call a sister in recovery, call a brother in recovery, call a trusted sponsor, therapist, adviser, call the national confidential twenty-four-hour gambling hotline, 1-800-522-4700—call *anybody!*

8/15/09: I've worked for hours. I wrap up a chapter. I want a reward and think, Why not check into my favorite free online slot? I make myself pick up the phone and call Jackie from my GA meeting. She's not home. I figure that's a sign to just go ahead and play. Somehow, I remember the "hole in the street poem" and call Nora in the Mojave. She answers. I say, "Damn, I was kind of hoping you wouldn't pick up the phone." "Got the jones?" she laughs.

I laugh and feel the jones evaporate.

3. Create a day—one day at a time—in which there is no money or time to gamble.

5/22/09: I woke up antsy. I take all my cash except for $20 and deposit in the bank. I take my credit cards to Larayne's house. She agrees to hold them for me till the jones passes.

I gather up my wash and go to the Laundromat. While I'm waiting for the clothes to dry, I call Candace. She works graveyard, and she's home and awake. We make plans for a twilight hike in Joshua Tree.

4. Exercise—swim, go to the gym, ride your bicycle, do yoga or Tai Chi, a martial art, a dance class, whatever will get you off your seat and out of your head. If you can't afford a private pool or gym, there may be a public one in your town. If you can't afford a bicycle or yoga lessons, walk.

9/4/09, 3:30 PM: The magazine hasn't sent my check yet. Yet! I dropped my favorite old blue bowl on the kitchen tiles. I just learned my friend in Ohio has breast cancer. The dog next door has howled for an hour straight, as he did yesterday and the day before. All I have to do is click on Free Slots, U.K., and I can smooth down the sandpaper in my brain. I'll do it after I take a walk.

5:00 PM: As always, twenty minutes into walking, I felt my head start to clear. I came back five minutes ago. I read my entry from an hour and a half earlier, and the urge to play online slots seems like a mirage.

If you try everything and cannot resist, you are not alone. There are, after all, only three kinds of gamblers:

those who've slipped,
those who could slip,
those who could slip again.

Every one of us in recovery is in a huge circle with you. If you have found yourself perched in front of your slot machine—and are a stronger woman than I am—you might be able to pry yourself off the slot machine seat and make a call to the gambling hotline or a friend. If you can't, when you finally come home, pick up the phone. Call a friend. Call another friend. Call the gambling hotline in your state or the national, confidential, twenty-four-hour hotline: 1-800-522-4700.

Hearing another voice may break the spell. Most of us will find ourselves still in a state of intoxication for at least twenty-four hours after we play. During that time, we think with an altered brain. We make the same "decisions" that we do when we are in a gambling run. If we can talk with someone long enough to rewire at least a segment of our brain, we can begin to think clearly.

3/30/09: Escaped this time. Good enough for now. I couldn't have stopped myself from gambling this morning if I hadn't heard the voices of Larayne and my friends. In fact, in the old days, I would have sat in my motel room trying to think of anything but that red sign—and I would have most likely headed right back to wreak vengeance.

I've recently gotten involved with an online gambling addiction support group. I hit it off almost immediately with a recovering woman in Great Britain. She was hanging on by her fingernails and slipping frequently when we first connected. Now she's staying clean. She wrote recently of a typical day in her nongambling life. It is a perfect template for any addict battling relapse:

. . . it's the memory of consequences that eventually keeps us safe once we start our recovery. It's when we forget that we are in jeopardy. "Lest we forget"—another good mantra.

I scored again today by not gambling. I went through my usual daily paces—soy cappuccino before work, roast veggies for lunch with a walk to the bank to deposit a small cheque, then back to work—and after work I bought some Turkish dried apricots, a Danish pastry for my mum, a jar of organic tahini, and then traveled home.

The tram stopped in front of that venue for the connection with the second tram of my journey, which takes me on the last leg close to home. I stood in front of the venue doorway again across the road and had no urge. It was so unlike how I was feeling most of the past year until just a few weeks ago. I had been unable to resist crossing the road and going inside until recently. Before then I had often been in that spot across the road, tossing up yes or no and then promising myself to only bet $2 or $5 and following my thoughts across the road and through the dark doorway. At first I was true to my promises to myself, but then sooner rather than later couldn't leave without putting everything I had with me into the slots.

When I began entering those doors I cannot recall. I don't know if it was this year or last. The important thing is I don't feel I want to go through that door again, and it does feel firm. It seems I have a steadfast commitment, and I would bet my bottom dollar on that. :-) But one can never be too sure. Lest we forget.

When I look through those doors I think and contemplate those experiences when I walked out after I'd gambled for hours and felt somewhat shattered, emotionally slipping out of reality. . . .

The days that followed each of my slips left me feeling uncomfortable with myself, edgy, my focus on what was the purpose of my *life a bit chipped away. I guess this withdrawal with my recent slips was relatively mild compared to how it used to be in my deep binge-ing days gone by. It was either continue tolerating these milder but unpleasant experiences or cold turkey abstinence. I think cold turkey abstinence is the only way we can do this, although some people argue with me and say gradual giving up is best.*

There is no gradual giving up for the true gambling addict. There is only cold turkey, maybe once, maybe as many times as it takes. And most women in gambling recovery cannot do cold turkey alone. As I remind myself again and again—every day—I know I can't.

IT'S A FAMILY AFFAIR

Studies have shown that children of pathological gamblers are more prone to becoming gamblers themselves. Eighty percent of teens with gambling problems had at least one parent who gambled, according to the Pathological Gambling Report. With the rise in Internet gambling, it is becoming easier for your children to model their behavior after you and become pathological gamblers themselves.

—Leslie Davis, CRC Health Group

I live alone. There is no partner. There are no children or grandchildren who rely on me. My mother and father are dead. My brother lives 2,700 miles away. We speak a few times a year. I have no connections with extended family. And yet, when a GA member reads the thirteenth question in our Twenty Questions, "Did gambling make you careless of the welfare of yourself or your family?" I answer, "Yes."

229

It will be years, long, clean years, before I will know just how severely my compulsive gambling affected my ability to love. Even now I suspect that as I drew into the smoky cocoon of the casino, I began to pull further and further away from those I cherish. I found ordinary moments with friends and family boring. In the last eight or nine years of my gambling compulsion, I became increasingly irritable, quick to judge, quick to resent and blame.

My three adult children know that I am a gambling addict. We have worked hard over the years to become accepting of each other, and in that acceptance, we are friends as well as family. They know that if they are visited by troubles or distress, I will listen. Only listen. They know I believe that they are each the keepers of their own lives.

I left my old home in Rochester, New York, and my grown children in 1985. I had learned by that time that I would need to create new kin—a family made up of friends. I moved to Flagstaff, Arizona, a town in which I knew no one, a place that provided a social emptiness that would allow me to find a new self. In less than a year, I became part of a familial web of friends—writers, activists, river runners, rock climbers, poets, musicians, buddies, acquaintances, and soul mates. By the time I left Flagstaff in 2008, the web had frayed. I don't know how much of the thinning out was natural attrition and how much was the change in me—changes brought on by intemperate love affairs, one with a man, the other with gambling. I do know that by that time, I had become an irritable, emotionally myopic, and blaming woman.

I write from inside the addiction—without the surround of a kinship circle. Still, what I have learned from other women in Scheherazade's Sisters and GA, from their loved ones—and about my responses to my friends' concerns about my gambling—may be of use to families and friends who suspect or know that a loved one is disappearing before their eyes into endless wagers for comfort and excitement.

You may be the partner, child, grandchild, mother, father, sister, brother, or friend of a gambling addict—and you may not know it. There may be mysteries in the world you share with the addict: unexplained absences; missing bank statements and credit card bills; increased anxiousness, mood swings, and irritability in a family member or friend; a brilliant student flunking her favorite classes; at the most extreme stages, phone calls from creditors—and strangers, cold-voiced strangers (people to whom the gambling addict owes money). It is not uncommon for a partner to suspect the gambler is having an affair. And it is not uncommon for others to not know the seriousness of an addict's compulsion until too late.

When I first began writing about gambling addiction, I received a call from a woman who lived in the town where my "neighborhood" casino was located. She asked to talk with me. I asked her what about. "The casino," she said and burst into sobs. I waited till she could speak. She told me that she had just returned from her eighty-two-year-old mother's funeral. Two days earlier, a neighbor had become suspicious when she had not seen the mother in her garden for a few days.

The daughter had raced to her mother's house, pounded on the door, and when there was no answer used her spare key to enter. Her mother lay dead on the living room couch.

There was an empty bottle of antidepressants next to her and a folder on the floor. "I was so shocked that I didn't even call for help. I dropped to the floor next to my mother's body and picked up the folder. My mother's handwriting was on the front. When I saw her writing, I started to shake. Inside the folder were eleven current credit card bills. She'd put them in careful alphabetical order. They were all maxed out. None of them was for less than $5,000. On the front, she'd written, 'I am so sorry.'"

"Gambling," I said.

"We had no idea. Not my husband, my sister, my two brothers. We are a close family. We kids all live here or in Flagstaff, but I guess we've all gotten busy in the last few years. My brothers and sisters and I called every few days. I spent part of Sunday with her every week. Oh my god, I had no idea. Was I blind?"

I was speechless for a moment.

The woman cried softly.

"No," I said. "You might have had no way of knowing what she was doing. We gamblers become completely devious."

"My mother. A gambler. It can't be," the woman said. "But it was. You have to write about this. Something has to be done."

The woman called me a year later. Her mother's death had jolted the family into a new commitment to being in touch with each other. They met every Sunday for dinner and talk. "It turns out," the woman said, "my sister knew more than a little, but even she didn't know how bad it had gotten. None of us knew until we started going through the records.

"My mom had taken out a second mortgage on the house and lost all of it. The bank was going to foreclose. She'd eaten up all her savings, all the investments my dad left her, and she'd taken out about $800 in those payday loans.

"But here's the strange part—it's so bittersweet. It turns out that my sister had been gambling with my mom, two or three times a week. She hadn't told anybody. She had a nest egg my dad had left her, and she's always told her husband that it was her money and she was keeping it to go back to school someday. So, he had no idea what was happening. The nest egg is gone.

"That first terrible day we got together, my sister told us all the truth. She found a GA meeting in North Phoenix she goes to every Friday night. So, my mother's death had two positive effects. My family is growing closer. My sister may not take the same path. But neither of those can stop the hurt I feel every day—or the guilt that I didn't pay closer attention and do something."

"There may have been little you could have done," I told her. "And no matter how much your mother loved all of you, she crossed a line. After that there was nothing she could do."

Perhaps the hardest fact many loving families and friends have to face about the compulsive gambler is that there is often little or nothing they can do to help. Nora has told us in the circle that her partner, Jen, knew what was happening. Nora opened up to her. They worked out strategies and agreements. And Nora broke every one of them.

A few of my close friends knew how much I was gambling. My youngest son knew. They were also people who dealt with their own compulsions, so they knew what it took to stop anything alluring and addictive. They knew that if they told me I might want to slow down, I'd go faster. They knew that if they offered to be a recovery buddy whom I could call when I felt the impulse, I'd never pick up the phone. They knew that no matter how much they cared about me, their caring couldn't penetrate my fierce need to gamble; my denial—"I'm okay. I didn't lose that much. I'll hold off for a few months."—or my lifelong determination that "nobody would be the boss of me." The best thing any of them ever said to me was, "I'm worried by how much you're gambling." I had no glib answer for that concern.

So, at the same time that true gambling addicts are powerless over the urges and impulses their brain spits out, the people around them may be equally powerless to help. Still, there are methods by which family and friends can take care of themselves—which may be, in the long run, the most healing actions of all. Family system theorists have long taught that any collection of close-knit people is a whole entity. When one element of the entity is in trouble, the entire system is in trouble. And it is possible that those who might not identify themselves as "addicts" may suffer from equally destructive compulsions.

To more deeply understand how a family or friendship community can be part of a loved one's addiction—an active part—it helps to understand enabling and codependency. So much of what I might do to "help" an addicted friend can, in fact, be yet another trigger. Asking a friend if she is using; encouraging her to stop; saying—as well-meaning friends said to me—"Now, you hang on to that money you just earned"; actively monitoring the other person's behavior; sitting down with her for a good, honest "chat"—all of these can be invasive and controlling. And, all of those behaviors can stem from the "helper's" need for control. Addiction to the illusion of control lies at the heart of manipulation, perfectionism, believing one knows what's best for another person, compulsive busyness—the list of conditions could be a list of what are sometimes defined as "virtues" in contemporary culture: negotiation; getting all As; empathy; trying to be the perfect mom, worker, daughter. Co-Dependents Anonymous is a treasure trove of information about this control obsession.

Twelve-step programs have known this for almost as long as they have existed: Alcoholics Anonymous is aligned with Al-Anon and Alateen; Narcotics Anonymous with Nar-Anon and Narateen; Gamblers Anonymous with Gam-Anon and Gam-A-Teen. The "Anons" function as leaderless, nonhierarchical support groups—no dues, no fees—for family and friends of alcoholics and addicts, the "ateens" for the children of alcoholics, addicts, and compulsive gamblers. These groups operate on the basic principle that family and friends are as powerless over the addict as the addict is over the addiction. The Gam-Anon website states:

In Gam-Anon the member will experience relief from anxiety by accepting the fact of powerlessness over the problem in the family. The heavy load of responsibility for the gambling problem is lifted and the agonizing guilt in regard to failures is gradually alleviated. The energy wasted in attempts to stop loved ones from gambling can be channeled into more useful methods of problem solving.

The program suggests that we refuse to be responsible for the gambler's behavior, assuming responsibility only for that which is ours. The prevailing idea is, "The gambler will play as long as someone else will pay."

None of us want to face that there is anything in our lives over which we are powerless. The concept of the powerlessness that lies at the heart of recovery is the opposite of the modern Western cultural illusion that everything can be fixed and every distress can be overcome. And yet, what may seem a bleak and harsh take on a way to remain in loving contact with any addict can be a foundation from which to begin to repair lives. There are steps family and friends *can* take. There are maps and guides that can ease them along a difficult and rewarding path. Some of these aids come from Gam-Anon; some come from the expanding field of gambling addiction treatment.

We can't confront what we don't know exists. There are clues that may tell you that a loved one has a developing gambling problem or has become a full-blown addict.

Perhaps you and yours have visited Vegas on family vacations. Maybe you and a friend make a few trips a year to local casinos for a show, food, and a few hours of gambling. You play a few slots, bet a few hands of poker or blackjack, hit the dice table or the roulette wheel for 20 bucks—and stop. You're bored. You don't like the cigarette smoke and noise. You want to spend your money on something worth it.

You notice that Betty disappears. She shows up in her room a little after two o'clock in the morning. You don't think too much of it. Maybe she caught a late show. Maybe she needed some peace and quiet along the river. She doesn't say anything in the morning. You eat breakfast and head back home.

Then, slowly—or in the case of many slot players, astronomically quickly—there are changes in your loved one's behavior. If you are a partner or spouse, you notice absences—she comes home a few hours late from work, and there is always a good reason: a ten-minute trip to the store turns into four hours; an evening at the casino with her friends becomes an overnighter. She insists on paying the bills and doesn't want to trouble you with the receipts. She loses interest in lovemaking. She no longer wears the pearl necklace she once loved—the one her mother left to her. A friend calls and asks you if you're short on cash, because your partner just borrowed 300 bucks.

As you begin to understand what might be happening, you delicately broach the subject of her last two "evenings" at the casino. She tells you she is fine, she had fun, she only lost a couple hundred bucks and, besides, a few months ago she won a thousand. You want to trust her, but when you check your joint savings account, $1,500 has been drawn out in a month.

Perhaps you're the parent of a college student. She's dropped out of school and come home because, she says, "I need to find out what I really want to do." She works two jobs, but she spends every hour she's not working in her room. Often when you get up for a drink of water long after midnight, there is light in the crack under her door. You discover that the collection of vintage records you had stored in the basement is gone. You don't know about online gambling, so you suspect drugs. When you confront her, she says, "I don't know what you're talking about."

You are a friend. Your good friend asks to borrow money and pays it back. She asks again and pays it back. A few weeks later, she asks to borrow money and tells you it may be a month or so until she can pay you back. She becomes a little distant. You wonder about drugs. You wonder about her other friend, the one who always seems broke, whose moods swing up and down.

You know something is wrong, but you can't imagine what it could be.

The day comes when either the evidence has mounted so high that neither you nor your loved one can ignore it or the cold voices on the phone turn icy, the cop knocks on the door, your loved one's boss calls looking for her, you find the garage door locked and smell exhaust fumes seeping out—it's over. The fun—and the mystery—have run out.

Most wake-up calls are only beginnings. If your loved one chooses to admit her addiction, she still has more hard choices ahead. Some women dive immediately into a program of recovery—seek therapy, find a women's support group, join GA, or enter into a treatment facility. Others vow to stop. Some are able to do that on their own; most cannot. Some women quit for a while and then find themselves entrenched again in their compulsion. That had been my story for a long time, a story that could always resume.

If you find yourself faced with impassioned vows and broken promises from your loved one, you may want to consider organizing an intervention. While it is generally accepted in both twelve-step and therapeutic treatment circles that true addicts need to hit bottom before they can recover, interventions can sometimes interrupt the cycle of addiction before the bottom is reached.

An intervention is a process in which an outside therapist is brought in to work with the addict. Some interventions involve a drastic confrontation in the presence of family members and almost immediate transport of the addict to a treatment center. Many interventionists believe that this style of intervention can be damaging and less than useful for the long-term recovery of the addict. Most interventions are far more gentle processes.

The family first meets with a trained interventionist to plan the intervention. In that way, both the interventionist and the family can educate each other about how to shape the most gentle and effective process. The actual meeting with the gambling addict can then unfold as slowly and as thoroughly as is needed. The goal is for the addict to make her own decision to seek treatment.

There are many treatment centers that provide intervention services. There are also a dozen or more websites that offer intervention—some through treatment centers, some independently. The National Council on Problem Gambling is a reliable and ethical source of referral.

Most treatment centers offer programs for the entire family, usually a week out of the forty-five or thirty days the addict is in residence. A typical day in a typical week might include individual and group therapy (with the family itself, and with others there for family treatment) and presentations on the nature of gambling addiction and codependency and enabling behaviors. The recovering addict and the family will be guided through developing an aftercare plan once treatment is concluded.

Family and friends may discover that as they choose to accompany the recovering addict on her journey, they, too, are willing and ready to go deeper into their own self-awareness. Private and/or group therapy with a therapist trained in gambling addiction and family systems may be valuable. Books, information, and websites can be additional tools. Two free tools for anyone digging into themselves are a journal and a pen. I've kept journals since I was thirty-five. They provide reality checks, memories that are part of the structure and flesh of this book, and reminders that I am always in peril and I always make it through.

Private treatment programs, therapy, interventions, family weeks, and family counseling are expensive. Even with the best health insurance, they may not be within the range of most Americans. Public programs exist in many states that provide help for not just recovering addicts, but family and friendship circles. Google can provide you with dozens of resources.

A last caution. A last encouragement.

Beware of charlatans. There are many in the field of addiction treatment. A new friend told me recently of her former gambling counselor. He billed himself as a national expert. He charged big bucks. He was quick to hug her and hold her hand "in support," encourage her to call him on his personal cell phone, eat lunch with him. He told her and others in one of his support groups that they could trust him because he often visited the casinos "just to remind himself of how insidious they were."

Rather than throw money and trust away on a therapist or treatment facility that might turn out to be a vampire, turn to the National Council on Problem Gambling, the Council on Problem Gambling in your state, Gam-Anon, and Co-Dependents Anonymous for education and resources. You will not have to sign a dotted line or commit to a process or group that doesn't work for you, but you will find tools that can only help.

There is hope. I've been drawn all my life to alcoholic and addicted men—as lovers and as friends. I am a perfect candidate for Unavailable Narcissists-Anon. I never was able to change the behavior of a single one of those men. Through what I learned in

Co-Dependents Anonymous, Al-Anon, and Nar-Anon, I have been able to slowly, painstakingly change thinking and behavior for myself. I have learned that love cannot penetrate the shield of addiction. I have not failed in my ability to love.

DOWN THE ROAD

Suffering begins to dissolve when
We can question the
Belief or hope that there's anywhere
To hide.

—Pema Chödrön

October moves into Central Oregon. Gauzy clouds drift across a cobalt sky. The sunflower jungle in the front yard has gone to seed. I walk along the Deschutes River as early twilight settles in. Six geese fly across the face of a crescent moon. I look at the pale gold rushes along the river and think of the Mojave, of the desert grasses, the same gold under the same moon, and of the old Joshua Buddha that seemed to carry me till I could carry myself. And, I think of Scheherazade's Sisters and miss them.

A month later, I load clothes, road food, and a few jars of local marionberry jam for gifts, into the Vibe and head south. My son will watch the four cats. I'll stay with my friend Naomi in Reno. I'm already curious about how my heart and mind will behave when I drive down the slope into Reno and see the casino lights like dangerous and alluring galaxies in the high desert night.

I remember how hooked I'd been the last time Naomi and I had driven through. I'd felt my heart jump, my mouth go dry. I'd longed to say, "Please pull over. I'll catch you back at the house later." And I hadn't. The "how" of my choice to sit tight had been a mix of my time in GA and Scheherazade's Sisters, my affection for the people in those circles—and Naomi's nonjudgmental and loving presence.

By the time I drive down 395 toward Naomi's exit on this visit, it's six thirty, a new moon night, the sky obsidian. The casino lights call me. They always will. And yet, I make the turn to Naomi's house. We travel to the Thai restaurant via the long route. I stay put in my bed in her guest room all night and wake to the scent of coffee and fresh-baked rolls in the morning. I take the bypass route on my way out of town and head south.

A day later, as I step into the Scheherazade's Sisters meeting in Desert Hot Springs, I am greeted again by the scent of coffee and warm pastry. I think of women and good coffee; women and baking; women, nourishment, and comfort. Candace rushes forward to hug me. Someone else embraces me from behind. I smell a subtle perfume and know it's Delfina. I take a census of faces: Helen, Barb, Ginny, K-Siu, Nora. I don't see Sharon or Tiffany.

"Sharon?" I say. "Tiffany?" Delfina and Candace put their arms around me and walk me to the coffee room. "Fortify yourself," Candace says. "There's bad news and good news."

"What?"

"The bad news is that Sharon blew a weekend in Vegas, then four nights a week for a couple months in the casino in Indio. The good news is that she's in treatment up in Redlands. She'd be with us, but she can't leave the treatment center for another two weeks, but you can visit.

"We'll let Tiffany tell you the other good news."

We go into the circle. A new woman hesitates at the edge of the circle, then takes a seat. She is dark-skinned, sad-eyed, her gleaming black hair gathered into a long ponytail.

Tiffany races in the door and skids to a stop. "Mary!" she shouts. I take her into my arms. We've been back-and-forthing on Facebook. I knew she was keeping clean, but I'm delighted by the change in her. I remember the shamed and questioning mouse who'd crept into the room a half year earlier.

"You really came back!" she cries.

"For tonight," I say. "Maybe we could grab coffee tomorrow."

"After school," she says and grins. "I'm back in college."

Helen shoos us to our chairs, and we begin. "We decided to dedicate tonight to talking about how our lives are now," Barb says. "That'll catch us up with you and you up with us. But first, let's check in."

I've always loved hearing the check-in stories. We don't talk about gambling. We talk about the rest of our lives—the big deals and the tiny and ordinary. Tiffany's gone to summer school to finish freshman composition. Candace brought a rescue pup home from the pound. K-Siu and her parents are planning a trip back to the Vietnamese highlands. Helen's volunteering at the local library and turned down an invitation to join a Bunco group at the trailer park—"The gossip gals spread that I'm stuck up. They don't know the half of it." Nora and Jen are organizing a march in Palm Springs in support of gay marriage. Ginny's sister and brother-in-law and their three kids have temporarily moved in with her and her husband. "They fell for one of those bad mortgage deals a few years ago. Now he's lost his job, and she's been cut to part-time. So—we are famalee!" Delfina is pissed off at Elizar for checking up on her every time she goes out. Barb wishes there were somebody at home to check up on her—"Half the time, anyhow."

"Me," I say, "I am in love with my new home. The only thing missing are the desert twilights, the Joshua Buddha, and all of you."

The new woman has held back until we have all spoken. "I'm Celie," she says. "I waited because I'm not used to talking about myself. But I have to be here, and my rehab counselor says I have to open up. I'll try anything.

"You know what? It's almost funny. I'm a member of the tribe that owns those two big casinos down the road."

Candace laughs. "You owe me."

There is a tense silence, and then Celie laughs. "I owe *me*. I put every penny of my monthly casino profit check back into the slot machines. Every penny. Every month. And my husband did the same thing. And more on top of it."

"Do you want me to say something positive and encouraging?" Ginny asks drily.

"Anything but," Celie says. "Just tell your stories. That's how my gran taught me and my brothers and sisters. She said that's the only thing that gets through to pig-headed kids."

"I'll start," K-Siu says. "I am so thankful for how good my life is now—and sad that it took me so long to understand how bad it had gotten. When my mother and father saw how well I am doing, they decided to take me back to visit Vietnam. They want me to stand on the ground of my homeland. They believe there is more healing there for me.

"They trust me now. My mother said she had wondered for a long time if something she had done wrong in their village had brought a curse onto me. I told her what I have learned here. She said prayers, and a few days later told me that she understood that she had not been the cause of my troubles.

"And then I had a dream about the family things I had sold to the art dealer. They turned to smoke in front of me, except for a blue and red weaving. One of my aunts was a woman who could tell you what dreams meant. She is long dead, but when I woke I knew what my dream wanted me to do. Maybe I inherited something from her.

"I went back to the art dealer. The blue and red weaving was in a glass case. There was no price tag on it, but I knew it would be very expensive.

"I told the man I hoped to buy back the weaving. I said that I could give him a little every week until it was paid for, even if it took ten years. Then, I told him the truth. You know that when I first came here I was sick from all my lies. I am learning with you that honesty will keep me from gambling again. The man listened.

"He unlocked the case and took out the weaving. He put it in my hands. 'I will sell it back to you for $100 more than I paid you. I am getting old. I have no children. I have more than enough. Take the weaving home with you. My brother died in the highlands. He'd want me to do this.'

"I paid him $50. I told him it would take a while to pay him back and that I would bring him $50 every week. I began to thank him. He stopped me. 'No,' he said, 'I want to thank you. You have given me something I didn't know I needed until you told me your story. You have given me honesty—and a way to thank my brother for everything he taught me. Please take the weaving now. I know you'll be back.'"

K-Siu opens her carrying bag. She pulls out a bolt of indigo cloth. There are designs woven in red. "My great-uncle made this. You'll remember that the men weave in our culture." She hands it to Helen, and we pass the cloth around the circle.

When it gets to me, I trace the designs with my finger. There are a fish, a bird, and clouds with rain. I remember a former love who had fought alongside the Montagnards. I hear his voice: "The red dirt up in the highlands was just like here in the Verde Valley. When the monsoons hit that red dirt, we looked like we had slogged through a river of blood."

I hand the cloth back to K-Siu. "We will take the weaving back with us to the highlands," she says. "There may be someone still in what's left of the village who can tell us more."

"How long have you been coming here?" Celie asks.

"A little less than a year," K-Siu says.

Celie is quiet.

"I'll go next," Candace says. "My story's boring compared to K-Siu's, but that's what's exciting about it. I wake up in the morning without being so scared I want to puke. I go to my kitchen, and there's coffee brewing in the automatic coffeemaker because of the electricity being on. There's food in the refrigerator. There's no automated voice from the bill collectors on my cell. I go outside and thank The Big Whatever for being alive.

"I eat, work out, catch up on errands, take a shower, and get dressed for work. My clothes are clean. They fit. I lost so much weight when I was gambling that I looked like a scarecrow.

"Five days a week, Wednesday through Sunday, I work one to nine at a job some would find boring. It doesn't particularly serve humanity or do anything much but earn my living. The customers are usually frantic about nothing. I'm polite.

"On my off-nights, I go to the community theater and rehearse. When I finally come home, I feel calm. I'm not terrified to check my phone messages. If there are bills in the mail, they are all up-to-date. I watch a little TV. The pup snuggles in my lap. I go to bed, and almost every night as I drift off to sleep, I think my life couldn't be better. How's that for goody-two-shoes!?"

Barb laughs. "I could handle that. I'm still shaky from my binge, but I can't forget when my life was one long binge—sleeping two to three hours at a time, stuffing myself with junk food, exhausted all the time. I'd wake up in the morning and think, *How am I going to get through all I have to do today?* The only thing that kept me going was the baby and the fact that I could jump on the computer to play online slots once I had the kid squared away and my dad was knocked out with his meds.

"Now? I still cram down cookies. I'm still zoned out on the computer after the baby and my dad are squared away—on computer Scrabble, Facebook, and a couple dating sites. Sue me! But I sleep okay, and I wake up at a normal time.

"I figure it's going to take a while for my brain to level out. And I know that my life has had too much 'Barb gives' and too little 'Barb gets.' Once I feel more solid, I'll start to take a look at that.

"I did learn something this time. If it wasn't for all of you and knowing I had a place I could come back to, I don't know that I would have stayed clean. And I had to be clean to realize that being pissed off is the strongest trigger for me. At least I got that out of my mess-up. And being clean allows me to feel. That's a mixed bag—I'm so mad about so much, and I am so lonely. But I figure the only way I can change my life is if I know what I feel and what I want to be different."

Helen nods. "I like what you said about being able to feel," she says. "Maybe that's the biggest thing for me. It was hard at first to feel. The folks at the treatment center seemed to set store by emotions. I told them I didn't have any.

"I've always been 'good old Helen never complains,' even when I was gambling. I grew up with the rule that children are seen and not heard, and I caught on fast that if I was quiet in school, I wouldn't get called on. I hated having to talk in public. And then when I married my husband, he did all the talking. All I had to do was smile and nod my head—and then do whatever I wanted to do.

"When I first stopped gambling, it seemed like everything inside me changed. I was nervous as a cat. I caught myself wanting to bite people's heads off. And cry? At the treatment center, I couldn't sleep most nights. I'd just lie in my bed, and the tears would run down my face till the pillow was soaked.

"My husband visited every other day. They made him come to some group sessions. He thought it was all poppycock. Still does. But one of the things I learned in treatment is that I can make my life as good or as miserable as I want to. So I pat him on the head and drive myself to my aftercare group and here.

"When the lady in the trailer park asked me if I wanted to join their little Bunco club, first I told her I needed to think about it—I learned that in treatment, too. I decided to go for a walk around the park and see what came to mind. Sometimes I'm lonesome. I often miss my gambling pals. They fell away when I told them I couldn't go to the casino anymore. You ladies are about 90 percent of my social life.

"I tried to imagine sitting with the gals while they played Bunco—just for the companionship. I knew I didn't dare play, and I didn't want to explain myself to them. I knew I had to tell the Bunco lady I wouldn't be joining them. It's always been hard for me to say no to anyone. I thought about not calling her back, but I guess I'd learned too much to let myself get away with that.

"I called her and told her I appreciated the invitation, but I wouldn't be joining the group. I hung up the phone and realized it was one of the few times in my life I'd honestly said no to someone without a long-winded explanation. In the old days, I would have said yes to that woman, made a plate of goodies, anted up, and pretended it wasn't real gambling. The second the meeting was over, I'd have scooted to the casino.

"If they think I'm stuck up, that's their problem. If I'm lonely, that's mine."

Helen pauses. "I wonder what would have happened to me if I hadn't started gambling and got in a big mess. I don't like to think about it. I wonder if I would have just faded away."

"I think about that, too," Ginny says. "I'm younger than you are, but I'd reached a point where I didn't look forward to anything. Now, even with my house crammed to busting with folks, and stretching my food budget to feed us all, I catch myself thinking about how I can make that sweet potato pie my nanny used to make—you know, how my family will be tickled to have a treat, and how maybe my sister and I can remember some of the good times we had when we stayed with Nans.

"She and I are talking. Really talking. It's been years since I had any real contact with my brothers and sisters. Sometimes it's hard, but I'd rather have hard truth than no connections. You know, it's only been a little while since I first came here, and I feel like it's been a century.

"I still get the jones now and then, but at least for now, it isn't walking my butt out the door to the casino. And things still aren't great between my husband and me, but I don't blame him. Maybe one of the biggest things I'm learning in here is patience. When you have to be the perfect everything, it can make you into a nasty woman. I was all sweety-sweet on the outside, but inside I was just waiting till I could head out the door for my gambling vengeance. And if my husband—or anybody else—got in my way, I was a bitch."

Most of us nod. I remember that for years, people had seen me as this big, warm earth mother and how I had hated being seen that way. I'd always known that despite the rushes of empathy I could feel for others, deep inside was a furious little girl waiting for her turn. I'd found my turn in the casinos. I'd loved the kindnesses (whether part of the job requirement or genuine) of other people cooking my food, making my bed, bringing me coffee, asking how I was doing. I loved feeling like a carefree kid.

Celie raises her hand. "I'd like to say something. This is my first time here even though I go to a GA group in Palm Springs. I made my last bet three weeks ago. I listen to you, and I wonder if I will *ever* feel okay again.

"I sit at home and try to watch TV. I can't make myself sit still. I don't have a job because my husband and I each get enough money from the casinos that there's no point in working. My husband is eating and eating. We don't drink because both of us had parents who were alcoholics. I'm scared I'm going to start eating like he does because I don't want to get fat like a lot of the other women are doing. Plus, we've got diabetes in my family, and I have to watch my weight, even though I don't want to. I love to eat.

"My kids are in school all day. They are starting to hang out with bad kids. I can't follow them around all day. So I sit and try to watch TV and hear my husband opening another bag of junk food and another can of pop, and I worry and worry about my children.

"Before the casinos came in, it wasn't like this. We were poor, but it seems our troubles were so much less."

She looks down at her hands, then makes herself look at us. "We can't go back," Celie says, "but I wish we could."

Helen reaches over and pats her hand. "In some ways, maybe we all wish we could go backward. I do. But being with these ladies, I've learned a lot. I do hope you'll keep coming back to be with us."

"I'll try," Celie says.

We take our break. I go out to the patio, my mind full of what I've heard. I need to be alone with the stories and my thoughts. I walk out through the back gate into the desert. It's dark. The lights of Palm Springs wash up pink into the sky. The stars directly above me glitter as though I stand on a northern mountaintop. I miss Flagstaff. I miss Everett and our desert road and gambling trips. I wonder what I will tell the circle. How do I tell them that I miss gambling every day? How do I tell them that I don't feel "happy, joyous, and free" for more than a few minutes at a time? How do I tell the truth and not scare Celie away?

The stars hold no answers. I hear footsteps behind me. "Want company?" It's Nora. I'm grateful for her presence.

"I'm thinking about what I'm going to tell all of you," I say. "I've been thinking that maybe I didn't lose enough to have really suffered—or maybe I'm just such a detached person. I don't want to scare Celie away. I want to offer up some hope."

"I know what you mean," Nora says. "We've had a dozen or more women drop in to the Sisters for a few weeks or months, and then disappear. I always wonder if it was something I said. I bet the other women feel the same way.

"We were freaked when we didn't hear from Barb. I wondered if I should have called her more often, if I should have met her for coffee, maybe told her more about how hard it was for me. I wondered if I'd made quitting sound too easy.

"But I also know the one gift we give each other all the time is our honesty. You and I know that nobody else can make a gambling addict gamble—or quit."

"I know," I say. "Maybe it's a good sign that I actually give a shit about another human being. Maybe, for now, that'll have to be good enough. And maybe caring about Celie includes knowing she's got her own path to find."

Nora hesitates. "What?" I say.

"You might want to consider something about how you feel. You've only got a few months clean this time," she says, "and you never had more than a year. I wonder if it's going to take some years for you to really feel what it is to live sober. It took me five years in NA before I could put two good days together—and then I dove into gambling."

She looks at me. "Don't you just want to smack me?" she says.

I narrow my eyes at her. "Yeah, but. . . . "

"Yeah, but," she says, "the night you told us your story you said that you thought you'd been using something from the time you were little and you'd never been clean all the way?"

"Yeah, but—exactly. So, maybe I'll add that to my progress report. It all counts in the long run. I sure am a weird combination of care too much and don't give a shit."

"Maybe most of us are," Nora says. "Jen's brother always says, 'Humans? Nothing but funny monkeys.' I hang on to that when I start thinking I'm responsible for everything."

Tiffany sticks her head out the door. "Come on in. We're starting."

Nora and I walk back inside. Somebody's put steaming mugs by our chairs, decaf for me, tea for Nora. There's a plate of pumpkin chocolate chip cookies. *Kindness,* I think. *Unasked-for kindness.* And nobody in Human Resources trained us how to be that way.

"If I don't talk," Delfina says, "I am going to explode. I wish I could tell some nice story like the rest of you, but I'd be lying. I haven't placed a bet in five years, but I feel as lousy as I did when I was in withdrawal. Elizar is driving me crazy.

"He's all the time checking up on me, and when I ask him nicely not to, he says it's because he loves me so much. You know what I think? I think he's fooling around. You know, how when a guy feels guilty, he starts accusing you of something."

"Women do the same thing," Nora says mildly.

"Funny monkeys," I say. Nora nods.

"You got that right," Delfina says. "But he's a big, dumb gorilla. And he's fifty-six. I know what that means."

Candace, Barb, Ginny, and I say, "Male midlife crisis."

"What is male midlife crisis?" K-Siu asks.

"A guy gets to his midfifties," Delfina says, "and realizes—*finally*—that he's not fourteen anymore. He goes *loco, muy loco,* and he tries to catch up on all the stuff he thinks he's missed: hot car and hot babes. My fool husband even bought himself a pair of those saggy B-boy shorts and some bling. It is pitiful!"

We're all quiet. Delfina shakes her head. Then she snorts and bursts into laughter. "Do you believe this? We're paying off the last of the bills. The kids are doing great. I'm all the way clean, *and* I don't dream about the *pinche cabron* anymore. And now this shit starts up. Men! I want a cigarette, and I don't even smoke."

"But you're okay, aren't you?" Barb says. "Even if he's gotta be a big fool for a while, you really are okay."

"I am. And you know what makes the difference, yes? Us, that's what makes the difference. Us women. I texted Ginny yesterday, and she told me to meet her for lunch. And then one of my cousins goes to Al-Anon. She called me because her husband has seen Elizar in his bad-boy outfit and figured I could use a little *chica* time. We did the only sane thing—we went shopping. And she brainwashed me with about an hour of Al-Anon medicine. You know, take care of myself. Let go. Take care of myself. Don't expect him to change. And take care of myself."

Delfina digs into her big purse and pulls out a deep turquoise suede clutch. "I took care of myself at Ross. Six ninety-nine for a forty-dollar bag. Retail therapy works."

Tiffany laughs ruefully. "That's wayyyyyy down the road for me. I'm going to be ninety before I'm ever out of debt. Between student loans—most of which I blew on gambling—and my credit card consolidation, I'm looking at no spare change for years. But, as you all know, my good news is so much bigger and cooler than my bad news.

"Sorry," Tiffany says, "I'll only go if you're done."

"It's all yours," Delfina says. "I got what I needed for now."

"First off," Tiffany says, "I want to thank all of you. When I went to bed last night, I felt like a little kid on Christmas Eve. I almost couldn't sleep, I so wanted it to be seven o'clock so I could come here and tell you stuff. I was lying there, and I realized it was the first time in a zillion years that I'd felt really excited about my life.

"It doesn't seem possible that nine months ago I was like totally numb. Or that I did some of the things I did to support my gambling."

Tiffany turns to me. "Mary, I told the group about the really gross stuff. They were really cool about it." She takes a deep breath and keeps going. "It was soooooo hard stopping gambling at first. I tried some medication, but it made me have scary thoughts, so I got off it. I was depressed and bummed, and I missed my old friends so much. My parents were nice to me, but I could see how scared they were. All I did was go to outpatient rehab, waitress part-time, watch TV, and make myself go for walks and write in my journal. I've got four full notebooks from that time.

"It took forever, forever, forever. But, one day I was watching some dumb soap opera and I realized I didn't care about any of it. I turned off the TV and went up to my room. I wrote for a while in my journal about how bored I was, and then I got bored of writing how bored I was. I went on Facebook. There was nothing new. So I logged on to the website of my old college. I started to remember how excited I'd been when I first was accepted.

"My mom came to the door of my room. 'Can I come in?' she asked. I knew she was trying real hard not to say anything. She'd gone to a couple Gam-Anon groups. I looked at her. The expression on her face—you know, the 'worried but understanding mom' expression that would have driven me nuts when I was gambling. This time I saw that she loved me. I told her to pull up a chair, and we looked at the college website together. When we were done, I said, 'I think I want to go back.' She didn't get all mushy or anything. She just smiled a little and said, 'That could be interesting.'

"My folks said I could live at home. There's a bus from the corner to my college. I signed up for just a couple courses. I'm still working part-time—and one of the things I learned in my outpatient group is that I take on too much, get stressed, and then I want to use.

"I'm doing okay in my classes, not A+, but I can remember things now. I do my assignments on time. I've gone to a couple concerts with kids from the outpatient program." Tiffany shrugged. "One of them is a guy. That's all—I'm done. You have to go now, Mary."

There is a moment of silence, and then we all applaud. Ginny holds up her hand. "Wait a second, Mary; we've got a little ceremony to do." She takes a gorgeously wrapped package from her purse and hands it to Tiffany. "It's from all of us," she says. "It's for your lit course."

Tiffany slowly unwraps the package. She coils the magenta satin ribbon and neatly folds the purple and green paisley paper. A note lies on top of the book inside. She reads, "And now there is a 1,002nd tale: Tiffany's."

"It's perfect," she says. She holds up an old, leather-bound copy of *The Arabian Nights*. She turns a few pages and reads

[Scheherazade] had perused the books, annals and legends of preceding Kings, and the stories, examples and instances of by gone men and things; indeed it was said that she had collected a thousand books of histories relating to antique races and departed rulers. She had perused the works of the poets and knew them by heart; she had studied philosophy and the sciences, arts and accomplishments; and she was pleasant and polite, wise and witty, well read and well bred.

"I hope I live up to this," Tiffany says. "Thank you, guys. I'll keep this forever."

She passes the book around. I wait till it gets to me and then tell the group, "Scheherazade didn't save her life alone. She told her new husband that she wanted to invite her beloved sister, Dinarzade, to spend a few hours with them before they became intimate. Dinarzade had been prepped to ask Scheherazade to tell them a story. And, so it began. Without Dinarzade's help, Scheherazade might have not been spared.

"It's almost too obvious to start off my story by telling you that you are my Dinarzades and I am yours. But it's true. I've been trying to think of how to say the truth. I still miss gambling in the casinos. I'm not often happy, or even content. But I couldn't come up with a plan, so I'll just say whatever comes to mind.

"When I first came here, I was less than a month away from my last casino bet. I was terrified—not of financial collapse, but of mental collapse. I had weird visual migraines, sometimes twice a day. I couldn't think. I couldn't find the words. I was so scared I couldn't even be angry—which I'd been almost every day for three solid years. I had lost my three best friends; my career—not my writing, but my career; I was tens of thousands of dollars in debt, and I couldn't have told you the exact amount. I'd lived in grime and clutter for years. I'd not really cared about my home, which I had once loved. I despised my own species—I would have said for how we are disrespecting and killing the planet, but I think now that my dull gray disgust came more from the damage I had done to my brain. I took pleasure only in what writing I was able to do and walking in the desert in the evening. I had no hope. I can't believe I wasn't suicidal, but I wasn't. Some tough little part of me insisted on living."

I stop. The advantage of letting my mouth run has always been that I learn something. I think about how crafting words is my biggest gift, and my biggest liability.

"Now? The migraines are gone. The terror is gone. I am still afraid, but my fears are the reasonable ones of an old woman growing older. My career has reemerged. I'll have two books out next spring, and I'm teaching a writing circle in a little indie bookstore in Bend. I write a twice-monthly column on writing for the local weekly. I've reconnected with one of my lost best friends, and our love is even more solid than it was. I find myself feeling more open to people, maybe even 1 percent less judgmental. I'm still in debt, but I'm a member of the working poor, so that makes me normal."

I catch my breath. I think about how I thought I would talk about the illusion of being "happy, joyous, and free" and how instead I'm hearing a woman talk about a life in which she is often happy, joyous, and free.

"I am such an addict," I say. "I listen to myself, and I hear all the components of a good life that so often I cannot really feel.

"I live in a sweet little house, and I care about it. I don't mind clutter, probably never will, but I can't stand the kind of grunge I once didn't even see. My mother must be spinning in her grave at those words!

"I am coming awake to goodness in some individuals of my species—that's grudging, but I can't not see all the damage we do to each other and to our home planet. I live lightly as I can on this earth—and do damage. Which brings me to the second-greatest gift of my imperfect recovery: I've rejoined the human species. The greatest gift is that I no longer fear my mind. That's it. That's who I am. Now."

"You're one of us," Nora says. "Just one of us."

"I've missed you," Helen says. "You're the first hippie I ever really knew. But when you get down to it, we're more the same than we're different."

"Thanks," I say. "I feel the same." I think not about the gifts of my recovery, but of my using. Addictions are the great levelers. They create a democracy of misery and paradoxically can create a community of hope. It will always be a mystery to me why some of us—alcoholics and addicts—are blessed to land on our butts and find each other. It is not a mystery why we can sometimes be each other's only hope. The old '70s street wisdom comes back to me: *You can fool a fan, but you can't fool a player.*

I come out of my thoughts. Delfina tells us we need to figure out where we're going to meet Thanksgiving week because the center is being closed for new carpeting. Barb hands out flyers for a women's addiction retreat. We close the circle. We all take our cups to the kitchen. Candace fills the sink with soapy water and washes them. Helen passes the last of the cookies around.

I talk with her, with Ginny and K-Siu and Candace. I don't want to leave. I remember how I had once sat engrossed in groups and twelve-step meetings only to flee the instant the formal gathering ended. Barb asks me to join her and Celie for a late dinner. "I'd love to," I say. We head out into the soft desert night.

I meet Tiffany for coffee the next day, then drive to the treatment center to visit Sharon. In some ways, I have felt closest to her during my time with the Sisters. Our sarcasm, our mordant awareness of our absolute fallibility, the way she spins out words into seductive stories—and spins them into herself, into the webs that have so often held her fast.

We sit on the patio. She lights a cigarette and shrugs. "These are what's left. No more terminal exercise. No more bingeing and puking. No more cocaine. No more blaming Bob for why I can't or why I have to. No more unbearably gorgeous and dry-mouthed drives to the casino. No more."

She pauses. "So how's tricks, sister?"

"The same. My version. No more teaching narcissists how to love. No more pretending I can get away with eating myself into a coma. No more drowning in anything that will buy me a little break from my good life. No more walking up to the big glass doors, seeing the fairy lights inside, and going into that place where it seems like five minutes has passed and I've aged ten years."

"Yee ha," Sharon says.

"Did you hit the big wall?" I ask.

"You mean where I face that I'll never be able to play innocently again?" she asks.

I nod.

"I did. You, too?"

"Yes. My longtime road pal, Everett, says that's 'when the toy finally breaks.'"

"And now?" Sharon says.

"I'm talking with my friend," I say. "I'm telling her I miss her and I miss Scheherazade's Sisters and I'm grateful there's a GA meeting up in Bend. I like my life better. I'm probably going to the little mom 'n' pop Thai place in Joshua Tree for dinner, and then I'm going up on the mesa to hang out with the Joshua Buddha while the sun sets.

"And you?"

"I'm talking with my friend. She knows I miss her. I'd tell her that I'd come and visit up north, but I can barely think about the next five minutes, much less that far ahead. I'll go to my Family Group, then dinner, where I'll make myself eat. After that, who knows?"

"Maybe this," I say. I pull a thick envelope out of my backpack. "It's all but the last chapter of the book. It would mean a lot to me if you'd read it and let me know what you think."

Sharon takes the package and holds it. "I will do that," she says. "I'll let you know."

A young woman walks toward us. "Gotta go," Sharon says.

We hold each other for a few seconds. "Down the road," I say. Sharon steps back and smiles. "Down the road."

I eat dinner alone. The Thai place I love has put out their buffet— chicken green curry; Buddha's Delight, fragrant with ginger; beef red curry; all of it home-kitchen soul food, far from hip-restaurant chic. I'm happy to sit alone by the windows. I watch twilight fade to silvery moonlit dark. The owner's son, a dignified and gracious teenager, asks if the food is good and suggests I get Pad Thai because it's just come out of the kitchen.

I remember the first time I ate here. I'd been clean a month. The migraines had held off that day, but the raw, obsessive thinking had begun to seep in. I forced myself to taste the food, dragged myself out from the maelstrom in my mind, and wondered if I was being taken toward the fate that had befallen my beloved aunt Mary, who had spent her seventies restrained in a nursing home wheelchair, her fingers busily plugging in ghost telephone connections as she had plugged in real connections in her job thirty years earlier. The young waiter had asked me politely if the food was good. I sidestepped the maelstrom and said, "Yes, it's perfect," and wondered if it was the last thing I would be able to speak—and if his quiet grace was a blessing.

On this November evening, I look out into the moon-drenched night. My mind is clear. The Pad Thai is just-right sweet and hot in my mouth. *Pay attention,* I think. *Carry these moments with you.* I'm only a little surprised when my fortune cookie reads: "Time, nature, and patience are the three great physicians."

I drive up the near-empty highway to my old cabin. The windows are dark except for one candle flame. I consider parking on the dirt road and walking behind the cabin to visit the old Joshua tree, the tree I had sat under every morning for almost a full year, saying my mantra and wondering whom I was praying to. I remember the two winter months of hard nights I'd sat in the dark, my eyes aching, my thoughts spinning in loop delay, and how even the light of a candle had been too bright to bear. I remember the silhouette of the old Joshua against the pale twilight and how it had been a comfort and an anchor. I wonder if there is another woman inside now, keeping a vigil with herself. If there is, I wish her comfort—and I can give her privacy.

So, I do not stop. It's enough to carry with me the memory of my first day at the cabin and how I'd pried rusted barbed wire and brads from the old tree and wondered if I would ever be free of the corroded longings I carried. I turn onto Winters Road and make a quick right. The dirt road is hard-packed and easy to drive. I pull off at the ruins of an old mining homestead and park.

The moon floods the dirt road. I recognize everything: the line of telephone poles, the osprey's nest on the one at the cross-roads, where I turn right and remember the soft pale gray and brown owl feather I'd found on an evening when the air had been ninety-four degrees. I stop. I see the shape of a seated man in a clearing in the Joshua trees. He gleams faint pewter. I walk slowly toward him.

There are standing Joshuas to the south, west, north, and east. For at least 350 nights of one year I prayed in each of those four directions. I had no idea to whom I was speaking, to what— to perhaps the not even possible, perhaps only nothing. I had talked to the probability of Nothing as I had been taught, thank-ing the south for the little storyteller I carried in me; offering the west all that was in the way of my happiness; vowing to the north that I would stand solidly in my age; and facing the east, offering myself to what would come next.

Next carried me to now. Now I walk closer to the seated Buddha. I skirt the last big creosote. In a breath, the man is the stub of a big branch on a huge downed Joshua tree. If this is the 351st time I have visited the tree, this is the 351st transforma-tion. I greet the tree for the 351st time. Not bad for a woman spooked by commitment.

I sit on the fallen tree and let my breathing slow. The moon-light picks out a sliver of white in a crack in the Joshua bark. I touch the tiny spine. It is no longer than the first joint of my little finger, only a little less slender than a piece of twine. I remember the late July afternoon I'd found it. My first impulse had been to take it home. I am an addict. And then I'd known that there was no way to hold on to the wonder I had felt the instant I had bent to examine it and realized it was not a leaf or a scrap of bark, but the bones of a once-living creature.

I watch the moon arc up in the sky. I remember more: the December afternoon only a little less than a year earlier when I had brought myself to the Joshua, moving step-by-step through the maelstrom of thought, realizing about twenty minutes after leaving the cabin that walking was not providing its reliable medicine. I'd sat on the downed trunk and waited. It was the only thing I knew to do. If I thought even a millisecond ahead, there was only terror.

I waited and waited some more, forcing myself to stay in the moment. My thoughts had continued to loop back on themselves. I'd begun to tremble. A memory occupied me so thoroughly that the Joshua stump to my right and the far horizon both seemed phantoms. It was the old memory—*five-year-old me in my parents' bed, what should have been my mother in the kitchen crooning a wordless and eerie song. It wasn't her, though. It wasn't my mother's trained musician voice. And then I heard footsteps coming toward the bedroom. And I had disappeared into the coloring book I held in my small hands.*

I had snapped myself back into my shaking body. I knew what I had never known before. My mother had not been simply a bipolar depressive. She had been psychotic. And when psychotic, had disappeared from herself. I had been motherless—not always, but often enough to have hollowed me out. If it had been only her periodic absences, I might have healed. But the psychosis had replaced the shape of my mother with an unknown and dangerous creature. I had fled to the only shelter I knew—inside my mind.

I had sat with the knowledge. I'd somehow known to let my body run what happened next. The shaking deepened. It wasn't enough. I had made a tiny sound and choked it off. The great silence of the desert held me. I had whispered, "Help." I'd felt the solid trunk of the Joshua beneath me and held my hands out in front of me. The moon had gleamed on my skin.

"Help," I had said. "Help. Somebody please help me. Please. Please." My voice had risen to a wail. I'd slid to the cool earth and leaned back against the Joshua trunk. I had cried out again. The shaking had become shuddering. I had longed for the tears I had not cried for too long. They did not come. I let them be. Slowly the shuddering eased. I'd pulled myself to my feet and sat back down.

I had waited. As slowly as the trembling had ceased, words began to form in my mind. They were simple, and they made sense. "Thank you." I whispered them. "Thank you. Thank you, Mom, for your courage. Thank you for my delicate brain. Thank you for a home filled with books and music."

I had not known that my shaky gratitude had been a beginning.

"Nature, time, and patience . . . " I whisper the words, and they bring me back into the present. I slide down again to the cool sand. "Thank you," I say. I think of friends who had bailed me out again and again, in acts of generosity that the rules of politically correct psych theory would label "enabling" and the rules of something more ancient would label "lifesaving." I thank each of them. I think of the years of free therapy that gave me little islands of comfort and order in a Sargasso Sea of addiction and obsession. I thank all of it: my genuinely loving therapists and the casino money that funded the programs. I think of the miraculous intersections of people and spiritual practices that brought me to my dangerous friend, the unveiled Mahakala, and I thank them.

And then I stand, and I turn in the four directions—to the pale sand and the moon-silvered mountains. "Nature, time, and patience," I whisper, "thank you." I touch the tiny spine. I wrap my arms around the old stump. "Thank you," I say. "You have saved my life."

Then I head out down the road—toward home.

RESOURCES

YOU NEED HELP AND YOU WANT IT NOW

National gambling addiction hotlines:

National Council on Problem Gambling: 1-800-522-4700
Gamblers Anonymous: 1-888-424-3577

Online Support

Gamblers Anonymous: www.gamblersanonymous.org
Gamblers Anonymous Victoria: www.victoriaga.org
This website is packed with practical information, including the most inclusive list of symptoms of withdrawal.
Gam-Anon: www.gam-anon.org
National Council on Problem Gambling: www.ncpgambling.org
Women Helping Women: www.femalegamblers.info

YOU WANT TO LEARN MORE

The Internet is a treasure trove of information, encouragement, and connection for the woman gambling addict. Simply Google "gambling addiction," "women and gambling addiction," "gambling addiction treatment," or any theme specific to you.

Caution: More than a few casinos and online gambling sites tuck their advertisements away in some of the sites that are specifically designed to help you. If you are easily triggered, know you sometimes may have to navigate through the minefield.

The Wager: www.basisonline.org/the_wager

An up-to-date professional journal of articles on gambling addiction research and treatment, many of its articles easily read by the layperson.

Books

Anonymous. *A Day at a Time: A Book of Daily Meditations for the Compulsive Gambler.* Center City, MN: Hazelden, 1994.

Currie, Billye B. *The Gambler: Romancing Lady Luck.* Toronto, Canada: Inner City Books, 2007.

Davis, Diane Rae. *Taking Back Your Life.* Center City, MN: Hazelden, 2009.

Gamblers Anonymous. *Sharing Recovery Through Gamblers Anonymous* (a.k.a. *The Blue Book*). Los Angeles: Gamblers Anonymous Publishing, 1984.

Lancelot, Marilyn. *Gripped by Gambling.* Tucson, AZ: Wheatmark, 2007.

Perkinson, Robert. *The Gambling Addiction Patient Workbook.* London: Sage Publications, 2003.

WORKS CITED

INTRODUCTION

Collier, Gaydell, Nancy Curtis, and Linda M. Hasselstrom, eds. *Crazy Woman Creek: Women Rewrite the American West*. Boston, MA: Mariner Books, 2004.

National Council on Problem Gambling. www.ncpgambling.org.

Problem Gambling Services. "About Problem Gambling." Connecticut Department of Mental Health and Addiction Services. www.ct.gov/dmhas/cwp/view.asp?a=2902&q=335212.

CHAPTER 1

Arabian Nights, classic illustrated 8th ed. Gilberton Publications, 1943.

CHAPTER 3

Blum, K., et al. "The D2 Dopamine Receptor Gene as a Determinant of Reward Deficiency Syndrome." *Journal of the Royal Society of Medicine* 89 (1996): 396–400.

Breiter, H., et al. "Functional Imaging of Neural Responses to Expectancy and Experience of Monetary Gains and Losses." *Neuron* 30, no. 2 (2001): 619–639.

Comings, David E. "The Molecular Genetics of Pathological Gambling." *CNS Spectrums* 3, no. 6 (1998): 20–37.

Denizet-Lewis, Benoit. "An Anti-Addiction Pill?" *The New York Times*, June 25, 2006.

Kidman, Rachel. "Biology, Addiction, and Gambling: Dopamine's Many Roles." *The Wager* 8, no. 38 (September 17, 2003). http://thedram.org/backissues/2003/vol8pdf/wager838.pdf.

McManamy, John. "Dopamine—Serotonin's Secret Weapon." McMan's Depression and Bipolar Web (February 2008). www.mcmanweb.com/dopamine.html.

Pate, Lori. "Dopamine, Drugs and You." MedHelp (May 27, 2008). www.medhelp.org/user_journals/show/11839.

Petry, Nancy M. *Pathological Gambling: Etiology, Comorbidity and Treatment*. Washington, DC: American Psychological Association, 2005.

Shaffer, Howard J. *Expressions of Addiction*. Online photographic exhibit. www.expressionsofaddiction.com.

Volkow, Nora D., et al. "Association of Dopamine Transporter Reduction with Psychomotor Impairment in Methamphetamine Abusers." *American Journal of Psychiatry* 158, no. 3 (2001): 377–382.

———. "Cocaine Cues and Dopamine in Dorsal Striatum: Mechanism of Craving in Cocaine Addiction." *The Journal of Neuroscience* 26, no. 24 (June 14, 2006): 6583–6588.

Wurtman, Richard J. "Neurotransmitter." Microsoft Encarta Online Encyclopedia (2008). http://ca.encarta.msn.com/encyclopedia_761586355/Neurotransmitter.html.

CHAPTER 4

Aasved, Mikal. *The Psychodynamics and Psychology of Gambling.* Springfield, IL: Charles C. Thomas Publisher, July 2002.

Blaszczynski, Alex, and Lia Nower. "A Pathways Model of Problem and Pathological Gambling." *Addiction* 97, no. 5 (2002): 487–499.

Currie, Billye B. *The Gambler: Romancing Lady Luck.* Toronto, Canada: Inner City Books, 2007.

Dixon, Mark R., and Kimberly Zlomke. "On the Need for a Behavioral Analysis of Gambling." Cambridge Center for Behavioral Studies, column posted April 8, 2002. www.behavior.org/columns/columns_dixon.cfm.

Dostoyevsky, Fyodor. *The Gambler/Bobok/A Nasty Story.* New York: Penguin Classics, 1966.

Ellis, Albert, and Catharine MacLaren. *Rational Emotive Behavior Therapy: A Therapist's Guide*, 2nd ed. Atascadero, CA: Impact Publishers, 2005.

Freud, Sigmund. *The Standard Edition of the Complete Psychological Works of Sigmund Freud*, vol. 21. London: Hogarth Press, 1961.

Griffiths, Mark, and Paul Delfabbro. "The Biopsychosocial Approach to Gambling: Contextual Factors in Research and Clinical Interventions." *eGambling: The Electronic Journal of Gambling Issues* 5 (June 24, 2002). www.camh.net/egambling/archive/pdf/EJGI-issue5/EJGI-issue5-feature.pdf.

Jung, C. G. *The Collected Works of C. G. Jung.* Edited by G. Adler and Hull R. F. C. Princeton: Princeton University Press, 1953–79.

O'Hare, Carol. Personal communication with author, 2009.

"Operant Conditioning." Basics of Learning, Macon State University Online Tutorial, 2004. http://tutorials.maconstate .edu/LEARNING/operant_conditioning_1.htm.

Petry, Nancy M. *Pathological Gambling: Etiology, Comorbidity and Treatment.* Washington, DC: American Psychological Association, 2005.

Schüll, Natasha D. "Escape Mechanism: Women, Caretaking and Compulsive Machine Gambling." Working Paper No. 41, April 2002. Center for Working Families, University of California, Berkeley. http://wfnetwork.bc.edu/berkeley/ papers/41.pdf.

Schüll, Natasha D. Personal communication with author, 2009.

Schwartz, David G. *Roll the Bones: The History of Gambling.* New York: Gotham Books, 2006.

CHAPTER 5

_____. "Escape Mechanism: Women, Caretaking and Compulsive Machine Gambling." Working Paper No. 41, April 2002. Center for Working Families, University of California, Berkeley. http://wfnetwork.bc.edu/berkeley/papers/41.pdf.

CHAPTER 6

Barnes, Lee. Personal communication with author, 2009.

"The Casino Experience." Signal vs. Noise, comment posted October 4, 2006. http://37signals.com/svn/archives2/the _casino_experience.php.

Executive summary on gambling limits, Great Britain Gambling Commission. www.culture.gov.uk/images/publications/gam blingreviewchapter1.pdf.

Friedman, Bill. *Designing Casinos to Dominate the Competition: The Friedman International Standards of Casino Design*. Reno, NV: Institute for the Study of Gambling and Commercial Gaming, 2000.

Rivlin, Gary. "The Chrome-Shiny, Lights-Flashing, Wheel-Spinning, Touch-Screened, Drew-Carey-Wisecracking, Video-Playing, 'Sound Events'-Packed, Pulse-Quickening Bandit." *The New York Times*, May 9, 2004.

CHAPTER 8

Lancelot, Marilyn. Women Helping Women. www.female gamblers.info.

"Memorable Quotes for The Man with the Golden Arm." IMDb. www.imdb.com/title/tt0048347/quotes.

"Withdrawal Symptoms from Gambling Addiction." Gamblers Anonymous Victoria. www.victoriaga.org/withdrawal.htm.

CHAPTER 9

Gamblers Anonymous. www.gamblersanonymous.org.

Hunter, Robert. Personal communication with author, 2009.

National Association of Cognitive-Behavioral Therapists. www.nacbt.org/whatiscbt.htm.

National Council on Problem Gambling. www.ncpgambling.org.

Petry, Nancy M. *Pathological Gambling: Etiology, Comorbidity and Treatment*. Washington, DC: American Psychological Association, 2005.

CHAPTER 10

Perkinson, Robert R. *The Gambling Addiction Patient Workbook.* London: Sage Publications, 2003.

"Withdrawal Symptoms from Gambling Addiction." Gamblers Anonymous Victoria. www.victoriaga.org/withdrawal.htm.

CHAPTER 11

Davis, Leslie. "Compulsive Gambling: You Aren't Just Harming Yourself." CRC Health Group, August 23, 2009. www.crchealth.com/articles/compulsive-gambling-you-arent-just-harming-yourself.php.

Gam-Anon. www.gam-anon.org.

National Council on Problem Gambling. www.ncpgambling.org.

GRATITUDE

The words "thank you" are not strong enough for my agent, Helen Zimmermann, a woman of extraordinary patience, and my editor, Brooke Warner, a woman of beyond-the-edges-of-the-universe patience. Without their guidance, I could not have written this book.

Keith Whyte, the director of the National Council on Problem Gambling, offered constant support—as well as limitless resources. Dr. Robert Hunter watched my back from afar, as did my trusted adviser, Larayne, and my brain-dancing pal, Ms. D. (both of whom must stay anonymous).

Thank you, Lee Barnes, my brother writer, for giving wisdom and insights gathered in years of being a gentleman in settings that were anything but civil.

I—and all women gambling addicts—owe enormous gratitude to Dr. Natasha Dow Schüll, whose pioneering work in how women gamblers *really* think was a jump start for this book.

Marilyn Lancelot was one of the first women to point me toward Gamblers Anonymous. Her website, Women Helping Women, kept me on track during what seemed like eternities of withdrawal.

Carole Seeley offered generous emotional and professional support, as well as friendship, which, now that this book is finished, I will have time to enjoy!

Matt, better known as Max, fed me in the last couple months of the intensive fine-tuning of the book—not just basic grub, but Thai curry, pot roast, and elegant anchovy pizza.

Michael Wolcott, as always, is my road and mischief brother and a spirit level with whom in conversation I can sometimes find a tenuous balance.

If I were still gambling, I'd show my gratitude to all the casino waiters and waitresses, busboys, cashiers, payout attendants, room clerks, maids, and card dealers—not with words, but with big tips.

But I would not be able to thank any of these people without the unfailing love and generosity of my friends in Northern Arizona and my family. You know who you are. You know you kept me going when I thought I'd be homeless and living in my truck. You kept me alive. To paraphrase the words of Don Marquis, author of the classic *Archy and Mehitabel*: to you, with you know what and you know why.

And to those two guys who sat down in January 1957 for the first "meeting" of Gamblers Anonymous, and all of you who sit with me in sisterhood and fellowship in Gamblers Anonymous circles: I owe you. I'll keep paying it forward.

CREDITS

INTRODUCTION

Portions of the Introduction have been excerpted from the essay "Slot Mamas," which appeared in *Leaning into the Wind: Women Write from the Heart of the West,* edited by Gaydell Collier, Linda M. Hasselstrom, Nancy Curtis (Mariner Books, 1998).

CHAPTER 2

"Twenty Questions" reprinted by permission of Gamblers Anonymous. http://www.gamblersanonymous.org/20questions.html.

CHAPTER 4

Excerpt from "A Pathways Model of Problem and Pathological Gambling," by Alex Blaszczynski and Lia Nower. Published in *Addiction*, Volume 97 (May 2002: 487–499). Reprinted by permission of Blackwell Publishing.

CHAPTER 6

Excerpt from Gary Rivlin's article "The Chrome-Shiny, Lights-Flashing, Wheel-Spinning, Touch-Screened, Drew-Carey-Wisecracking, Video-Playing, 'Sound Events'-Packed, Pulse-Quickening Bandit," as it appeared in *The New York Times Magazine* on May 9, 2004. Reprinted by permission of the author.

CHAPTER 8

Excerpts from "Withdrawal" and "GA 12 Step" web links reprinted by permission of Victoria Gamblers Anonymous. http://www.victoriaga.org

CHAPTER 9

Excerpts from the National Council on Problem Gambling are reprinted with permission of the council.

CHAPTER 10

Quote from the recovering woman in Great Britain is excerpted by permission of the original author, who wishes to remain anonymous.

CHAPTER 11

Information from Gam-Anon is reprinted by permission of Gamblers Anonymous.

ABOUT THE AUTHOR

Mary Sojourner is an NPR commentator and the author of *Bonelight: Ruin and Grace in the New Southwest*, an essay collection; *Solace: Rituals of Loss and Desire*, a memoir; the short story collection *Delicate*; and the novel *Going Through Ghosts*. She holds a master's degree in psychology from the University of Rochester. She lives and writes in Bend, Oregon, and is, for today, in recovery from gambling addiction.

SELECTED TITLES FROM SEAL PRESS

For more than thirty years, Seal Press has published groundbreaking books. By women. For women. Visit our website at www.sealpress.com. Check out the Seal Press blog at www.sealpress.com/blog.

Addicted Like Me: A Mother-Daughter Story of Substance Abuse and Recovery, by Karen Franklin and Lauren King. $16.95, 978-1-58005-286-3. A mother and daughter share their candid struggles with addiction—thirty years apart.

The Money Therapist: A Woman's Guide to Creating a Healthy Financial Life, by Marcia Brixey. $15.95, 978-1-58005-216-0. Offers women of every financial strata the tools they need to manage their money, get out of debt, and create a healthy financial life.

Girl in Need of a Tourniquet: A Borderline Personality Memoir, by Merri Lisa Johnson. $16.95, 978-1-58005-305-1. This riveting personal account gives us a glimpse of what it means to be a borderline personality in a relationship.

P.S.: What I Didn't Say, edited by Megan McMorris. $15.95, 978-1-58005-290-0. For the friend who's been there through everything, and the friend you've wished you could help, this thought-provoking collection of unsent letters expresses the unspoken.

The Chelsea Whistle: A Memoir, by Michelle Tea. $15.95, 978-1-58005-239-9. In this gritty, confessional memoir, Michelle Tea takes the reader back to the city of her childhood: Chelsea, Massachusetts—Boston's ugly, scrappy little sister and a place where time and hope are spent on things not getting any worse.

Purge: Rehab Diaries, by Nicole Johns. $16.95, 978-1-58005-274-0. An honest, detailed account of Nicole Johns' experience in an eating-disorder treatment facility, avoiding the happily-ever-after while offering hope to the millions struggling with eating disorders.